Cracking The Hospice Code

Your Nurse Advocates Debunk the top 10

Misconceptions of Hospice

By

Linda Kritikos, R.N.

Pam Dunwald, R.N.

Contributions by Mary Droegkamp

© 2021

Your Nurse Advocate Consulting, LLC

Dedication

This book is dedicated to all the hospice patients and their families that we have cared for over the years. We as nurses have learned much from all of you. The experiences we have had the honor to be part of, have allowed us to grow as nurses and individuals. We are humbled by these experiences. Thank you for allowing us to honor your family members by sharing their stories. Your story may be just the one needed to help others dealing with the same concerns.

We would also like to thank all those that have contributed their perspective to this book. Without your contribution, this book would not have been able to bring forth the valuable insight that only you could provide.

The dedicated hospice nurses that continue to provide cares every day putting the needs of their patients ahead of their own. You are a dedicated professional and we are proud to join you professionally as the "The Nurse". We would like to thank our compassionate and dedicated husbands, families and friends for their support, sacrifices and encouragement. This has been greatly appreciated throughout the development of this book.

Thank You

Forward

Mary Droegkamp

I have worked in the healthcare industry for over 30 years. During my tenure I have had the honor and privilege of working and collaborating with a variety of clinicians- RNs, LPNs, Therapists, CNAs, etc. Their compassion, caring, and professional demeanor continue to move and amaze me. These clinicians have the innate desire to help others in their time of need. It takes special individuals to be able to do this day in and day out. The one fact I have learned over my years in healthcare is not every nurse can do the work necessary to be called a hospice nurse.

The traits that a hospice nurse possesses come from the heart; and can't be taught in school. These selfless clinicians are the embodiment of servant leadership.

How does a nurse tell a family their loved one is declining and it won't be long till they pass away? How do they selflessly continue to administer their care and compassion to patients day after day, knowing that no matter how much they minister their dedicated care; their patient will never get better? How do they explain what medications are best to use to make sure comfort is the number one goal in the dying process?

To say it is a difficult task to do all of this day in and day out is an understatement. The hospice nurse has one of the most emotionally draining and rewarding roles in the nursing field. Being a hospice nurse is a true calling. These nurses choose to be involved in this nursing specialty because of the hope,

support, and comfort that hospice provides

throughout the hospice experience beyond the

death of the patient.

Hospice nurses' gratification comes when they

see the care that they have provided results

in a patient death that is peaceful and

dignified, that meets the patient's needs.

Remember, the disease process has already

determined the "quantity" of one' life; hospice

enhances the "quality" of one's life for

however longer that is. Hospice nurses

consider it an honor and a privilege to share in

this very personal and private moment in an

individual's life. It is the greatest reward of

servant leadership. We all prepare for the

birth of a child, hospice nurses and the

hospice team prepare their patients and

families for the end of one's life. It is a unique position. Two of these hospice nurses that I have had the honor to work with, and that have lived this role are Pam and Linda.

Pam not only did the job of a hospice nurse but did it in a grueling rural area. Her stories are very different from the nurse who works in an urban area and had resources at her fingertips. Not only would her average drive be an hour on rural winding often unpaved roads; but she could also be called out in the middle of the night on these same roads if a patient needed her. There were many times she dreaded the car ride through the snow and unsafe roads, but she went because she knew her patient needed her. She prided herself in her knowledge of the dying process and what the patient and family needed both physically and emotionally. Her job satisfaction was complete when the patient passed peacefully and the family was grieving appropriately. She gave the patient dignity and compassion at the end of life.

Linda's belief in the hospice philosophy took her to one of her greatest adventures. She opened up a hospice company from ground zero. She was hired by an established hospice company to start a new branch and did that in a few short months. She hired and trained a group of clinicians that had the same passion as she did for the provision of excellent end of life care. Linda and her team's passion for excellent care grew that start-up company significantly in a few years. Her passion was validated by the quality scores she received from Medicare from the families she helped through the dying process.

Linda's expertise in healthcare operations and both of their long standing experiences in hospice, provide the validation for them to write about the hospice journey from a different perspective. They did not want this book to be a textbook, there are plenty of great hospice textbooks written. Their approach for writing this was more about the raw feelings and emotions that can be experienced during the hospice journey. This book provides anecdotal stories and educational insights. I was honored when they asked me to contribute to this book.

Pam and Linda are those nurses that will advocate for their patients with everything they have to make sure their patients have what they need to be comfortable at the end of life. Those needs may be as simple as a hospital bed, or more complex such as specific medication, or oxygen. If it will make the dying process easier or more comfortable, they will work tirelessly to try to obtain it. They are supportive, and knowledgeable in their approach. They will leave no stone unturned to obtain needed resources to meet the needs of the family and patient.

It was this passion that inspired Pam and Linda to create and develop "Your Nurse Advocate Consulting, LLC". A company with a mission to advocate for others through servant leadership. Pam and Linda want to put into action their diverse skill sets to assist others to make informed decisions regarding their healthcare choices. To provide recommendations for their clients to understand their options for care and treatment, to feel comfortable with the decisions they make, and to assist them to use their voice to advocate for themselves.

This book is just one aspect of the various levels of expertise these nurse advocates bring to the table.

Those who read this transparently raw and engaging book will learn from their experiences. You will know that hospice nurses and the hospice team go beyond their call of duty every day of the week. These nurses promote the hospice philosophy in everything they do.

Introduction

Pam and Linda

As patient advocates Linda and I both have experience with working in hospice. What we find is that most people lack an understanding of hospice and feel this is a service that is needed at those last few days at the end of life when no other options are available. In our book, "Cracking the Hospice Code," we share stories of enlightenment, courage, fear, anger, sadness, denial, and joy; all the emotions one can experience on the roller coaster ride of that final journey in life. It is our goal to share these stories and inspire you to take a more open-minded look at all the benefits of hospice and what it may mean for you and your family.

Hospice is a philosophy as much as a level of care. It is a choice that one can make when all the continued treatments and trips to the hospital become more of a burden. This may leave a negative effect on their perceived quality of life. They want to change the focus of their care approach. This individual wants to choose quality over quantity.

Part 1 of the book, we take you on a journey through the eyes of some of the most courageous people we have ever met. We share their stories of their hospice experience that eventually leads to the end of their life.

In Part 2 of our book, we address in depth the top 10 Misconceptions we have come across when people ask questions regarding hospice. We will provide information to dispel these beliefs and give you a picture of all the good things hospice can do. We will provide information for those looking at hospice as an option for themselves or a family member. Here is some food for thought. Have you ever said or thought about any of these things regarding hospice?

Hospice is only for the dying. You can't stay at home if you are enrolled in hospice. Hospice costs too much. Hospice doesn't care if they starve you to death. They just want to give you morphine and speed up your dying process. We will take you on a journey with several real stories and will address each of the 10 Misconceptions. In the end you still may not agree with hospice, but you will at least be well-informed!

We are excited to share this book and our hope is that you may shed a few tears, laugh a few laughs, and feel all the emotions as we take you on the hospice journey. We will do our best to answer your questions along the way.

We have also listed a consumer guides report in our resource list on the use of hospice care. This also gives you an unbiased look at what hospice is and how it may be of benefit.

If you or a loved one is in a position to be considering the hospice benefit, our heart goes out to you as we know this choice is not easy to make. Feel free to reach out to "Your Nurse Advocate Consulting," and we can assist you with any individual needs or questions you may have. Visit our website and get our free companion checklist "How to Know When Your

Elder Parent or Spouse May Need Help in the Home".

https://www.yournurseadvocateconsulting.com

This book was a stepping stone to the realization of starting our "Your Nurse Advocate Consulting" business. We wanted to find some way to take all the knowledge we have learned throughout our nursing careers and use it to help as many people as possible to navigate their way through our very complex health care system.

At this time, we want to acknowledge Susan Sly and members of her Agency 8 team Diana, Avery, and Jessica. Thank you for believing in us, and showing us that you are never too old to start a business! With your advice and coaching you helped us take all of this from a concept to a reality. We will

forever be grateful.

Sincerely,

Pam and Linda

Table of Contents

Chapter 1

"Hold On Wait a Minute, I'm Not Ready to Go Yet!"

Pam

Fear is real in this case. Mostly fear of the unknown. I know we are told that fear is not real. The old saying says FEAR is False Evidence Appearing Real. It appears real, it feels real, so it must be real. Not many people can say they have died before and can share what that feels like or what happens after you die. During the final journey the biggest fear we see is the fear of the unknown. What will happen to me when I pass? Is there Heaven? Will I go to Heaven? Will I be in pain? Will I suffer? This is going to be so hard on my family.

N.S. was my dad. You would think that having your oldest daughter as a nurse, your parents would be in pretty good shape and at least getting great health care and staying on top of their physicals and wellness check-ups. Not my father. I was the first one on his side of the family to go on to college. My dad graduated high school and went into the Navy and served during the Korean War. He met my mom at a party. My mom and dad had gone to a high school in Chicago and mom hung out with the "greaser" crowd. She was crying because her boyfriend had made her upset. My father was out of the Navy by now. Dad came in and rescued the day, swept her off her feet and they got married on her 18th birthday the year she should have completed her senior year and graduated high school. 10 months later I was born.

Dad was hard on us. Quitting and crying were not allowed. He had three girls before two sons came along and he raised us tough as nails. "Girls don't cry" we heard often. "My daughters are not going to be dependent on any man" he would bellow. Our dad was a good athlete and an excellent golfer and bowler. Losing was also not an option in our family. We are short statured, my dad was 5'6", mom 5'2" and none of us got taller than our father. My youngest brother is 5' 4".

One of the many sports the men in our family excelled at was wrestling. It was hard to sit next to dad at a wrestling match because he was just too intense. He felt every move as if he were on the wrestling mat himself. I seriously don't know who took a loss the hardest, my dad or the child or grandchild that lost the match .

I will never forget one day out in the front yard the neighborhood kids (we grew up on the northwest side of Chicago) and I were playing a game called Red Rover. Some people know it as Johnny Tackle or Monkey in the Middle. The object of the game was to tackle all the kids and the last one standing was the winner. All the kids would line up at one side of the yard and the person selected as "it" would stand in the middle. We would shout "Red Rover Red Rover let Johnny come over". Johnny would try to run past you and get to the other side without being tackled to the ground. If the person was successfully tackled, they joined you in the middle and you had another recruit to help you tackle some more kids. We must have been 7 or 8 years old and I didn't know my dad was watching out the window. It was a typical warm summer afternoon and we had our windows up to let in some fresh air. Next thing I know my dad comes out of the house and motions me to come over to the porch. I said "Dad, I am in the middle of a game!" He replied, Pam come over here please. So, I did and he said to me, "Pam, why can't anyone tackle that one boy. Why is he getting through every time?" I said "Dad, he is really wiggly and I can't tackle him." My father replied, "Pam, I want you to tackle that boy, do you understand me?" I sheepishly said "Yes, dad I will." He sat right there on that porch and watched. Here we go, "Red Rover Red Rover let Danny come over".

Danny ran towards me I am sure because I was a girl and also the smallest. I grabbed a hold of his legs and he was kicking and wiggling and trying to get away and I did it! I tackled Danny. As I walked over to my dad with a bloody nose he just smiled and said "That's my girl" took out his handkerchief from his pocket and wiped my nose.

Life was full of all sorts of those experiences growing up. As I grew up, I realized my father was just as hard on himself as he was on all of us. He wanted us to be the best we could be with control over our lives and wanted all of us to be successful.

Fast forward to nursing school. My family had moved to Wisconsin and I stayed in Chicago to complete nursing school. On my trips home to visit, I was always trying to practice my new skills I learned on anyone that would volunteer. "Dad, let me check your blood pressure". My father replied "No honey, that's ok I don't need my blood pressure checked." "C'mon dad yes you do" Now dad gets up out of his chair at the kitchen table and takes a step away from me and says "I said no, I don't need it." As I started walking towards him with my stethoscope and blood pressure cuff in hand, he started to walk away from me. "Dad, what's the big deal, I need the practice, let me check your blood pressure". Now he is walking around the kitchen table to get away from me! I followed him around the table a few times until he got angry and said "You are not going to check my blood pressure and that is it". I could see he was getting angry but I wasn't sure why. This was the first time I ever saw my dad act out of fear.

Several years later my dad suffered a mild stroke. He had never been to the doctor before that, not once that I know of. That stroke scared him so much that he went to the doctor if he sneezed wrong. He made a full recovery from the stroke, stopped smoking cold turkey and became a bit more health conscious.

By now I had moved away and was raising my own family. My youngest sister also became a nurse and later on completed her Advanced Practice in Nursing and became a Nurse Practitioner. We both noticed dad was starting to lose weight. We both knew what that could mean as sometimes cancer shows up as unexplained weight loss. We didn't know how to tell dad that we wanted him to get checked. He said he was feeling fine and not to worry.

His mom passed at the age of 62 from cancer that she kept from all of us until the day she insisted on going to her sister's two hours away. Grandma died at her sister's that night. All of grandma's siblings passed away from some form of cancer. We knew it ran in the family on my dad's side.

He eventually agreed to go to the doctor. Everything checked out except his blood count was a bit low and they didn't know why. His doctor was looking for something in his stomach or intestine that may be causing the problem. He had procedures that examined his whole gastrointestinal tract and nothing was found. Dad continued to lose weight and become weaker. Dad often had to get blood transfusions. We could tell he was in pain. Mostly back pain. Dad trusted the doctors and he did not want a second opinion. We learned later that dad had one episode with a couple of drops of blood when he urinated. We asked dad if they had ever checked his kidneys. They had not. Of all the diagnostics that were completed none were targeted for his kidneys. When they finally looked, they found a very large tumor on one of his kidneys.

This was a tough day for dad and our family. The doctors explained that there was nothing more that could be done because it was so advanced. Dad feared dying more than anything else. Our father insisted on having surgery to remove the tumor. Our annual family fishing vacation was planned and the soonest he could get his surgery was at the end of our trip. He insisted on going up north fishing. I drove him to the hospital for his surgery on our way home from fishing. I will never forget the surgeon's face of disbelief when he described how large the tumor was. "Almost the size of a football," he said. Dad didn't care he was not going to give up.

The outcome was explained as poor. Surgery would not prolong his life and the cancer had spread to his lungs. One of the hardest conversations I have ever had with my dad was to tell him to give up. That was not in his DNA nor in any of ours. I just wanted him to be comfortable.

Time passed and against his better judgement he agreed to enroll into hospice. He did it because we asked. He understood that no more trips to the hospital, no more blood transfusions.

Dad was enrolled in hospice for one day, when he became scared and he wanted to go to the hospital. Hospice was called and a nurse met him at the hospital and he signed off (revoked) hospice. He wanted whatever treatment he could get. He was so scared to die. He was so scared to give up. Family was everything to my dad. He was not ready yet.

My younger sister had been at the hospital all day with him and so my middle sister and myself took the night shift to stay with dad. It was late and his doctor came in to see him one more time and told him, "Neil, I am so sorry we missed your tumor. Can you forgive me?" My dad looked up at him and told him yes, it was o.k. That broke my heart to hear him say that because this was the first-time he sounded defeated.

Later that night we got one more glimpse of the dad we knew and loved. He called me over to the hospital bed and said he would like some sherbert. Orange was his favorite flavor. I pushed his call light and a nurse came in and as luck would have it, they had orange sherbert. I had to feed it to him. After a couple of bites, he looked up at me with that look he gives to you just before you knew you were going to get a spanking; and he yelled at me saying "Can't you slow down? You are feeding me too fast!" Some people might have been upset with being yelled at especially when you were trying to help someone, but my sister and I just laughed and soon dad was laughing too because this moment was as real as it gets. One more time we were with the same dad we grew up with and loved so much.

The next morning my sister and I talked to dad about going home. We have a large family with many children of all ages. We posed a question to dad; wouldn't it be nice to have your whole family with you and all together versus being in the hospital? He was reluctant to agree, but we decided to go home and he would accept hospice one more time. Plans were made for discharge and we took him home. We arrived at my parent's home mid-morning and got dad comfortable in the hospital bed. All the equipment was still there from hospice. They hadn't had enough time to pick it up after our father signed off (revoked) hospice services the night before. It was April 13, 2007.

Pastor came by around noon and dad was still responsive. He talked with the Pastor and made his peace with God and again accepted Jesus. My dad did not go to church much. His father, my grandpa was very involved with church and was a trustee however had some sort of falling out and wouldn't go back. We were the kids that got dropped off at Sunday School every weekend and picked up when it was done an hour later. As we got older and attended confirmation classes we would stay for church as well. I never really knew how my dad felt about religion but that afternoon he made it clear he would like to go to Heaven.

Shortly after Pastor left my dad became unresponsive. It seemed with his entire family around him there was no other business left undone that needed to be taken care of before he passed. The hospice nurse came about 4:00 p.m. a little frustrated with the "back and forth" situation but was gracious enough to sign him back into hospice as he lay there unresponsive. Most of the entire family was there. We sat around the hospital bed for more than a few hours watching and waiting. We sat vigilantly. I had been up all night and was exhausted and fell asleep sitting up on the couch. I woke to my youngest sister's nudge as she said "Dad has passed." I didn't hesitate one bit. I climbed into that hospital bed with dad, snuggled up to him, kissed him on the cheek and told him goodbye. I can honestly say that all of us being together with our father and

grandfather meant the world to us. We all
shared in an intimate family moment we will
never forget. Thank you, hospice for making
that possible for us. Till we meet again dad.

Chapter 2 Does the Devil wear Depends?

Dealing with Frustration

Mary

Imagine you are given a terminal illness diagnosis and told you have less than six months to live and there are no more treatments that can stop your disease progression. Where do you go from there? What do you do first? How do you begin to live the life you have left to the best of your ability? How does Hospice fit into the rest of my life?

They ask themselves if hospice means they are giving up and allowing death to come quicker. They have no control over the disease and death is an outcome they may not be looking forward to. The trained hospice clinicians see this time and time again when a patient is brought on for services. Truth be told, hospice care helps the family members just as much as the patient themselves.

Frustration is an emotion every patient will feel once they realize they are terminal and are not able to stop the inevitable from happening. It affects people in different ways, and sometimes in ways that are not always in the best interest of others! The following story captures this human emotion when dealing with end of life.

Richard was a husband and family man who didn't like to ask for help from anyone. It was quite the opposite for him in his extended family. If anyone needed any kind of help, it was Richard who was there to give it. No matter how far he had to go or how long it would take, he did what needed to be done. He was very stubborn. Richard would often leave his wife Alice, angry to go off to help other family members. Usually it was because someone else who should be doing it wasn't willing to go out of their way. Basically, Richard preferred to help others rather than asking anyone to help him.

Imagine you have worked hard your whole life and were able to steer your path of life for 68 years only to discover you are diagnosed with Stage 4 Colon Cancer. His options for treatment look grim. Which procedure is the less of two evils? What if you decide to do nothing? This is the situation Richard B. found himself in after he heard the words from the gastroenterologist. Adding to the mix was his anger at himself for not going to see the doctor. For months he neglected making an appointment while he had symptoms that he knew were not normal. Saying he felt frustration about the lack of power over his body is an understatement.

The unfortunate part is the people that felt the outcome of his frustrations were his family. Richard had a wife and five children during the time of his diagnosis. He told his family he decided to move forward with chemotherapy first. He would then have surgery to remove the shrunken tumor from his colon. Unfortunately, the cancer had spread to his liver. He would need to undergo another surgical procedure to deal with the affected area of the liver.

While Richard proceeded with the procedures, he had a large amount of anger at himself that would usually be directed as frustration towards his family. They just wanted to help. Being as independent as he had always been, his wife Alice was able to help during his treatments but it stopped there. He didn't want his children to see him as he declined and relied heavily on Alice.

As the months dragged on, she became more weary and exhausted from being the main caregiver. Chemotherapy was completed, and about two months later Richard had his surgery to remove the tumor. The blessing in this was, he did not need to have a colostomy after the surgery which was the worst fear he had since being diagnosed. The liver procedure appeared to have worked. Richard was stable during the several months of recovery. He was returning to a somewhat "normal" life.

Three years later, Richard was experiencing symptoms of pain and discovered the cancer had returned after a thorough exam. The cancer had spread into the liver and colon again. His decision to live out the rest of his life and have quality vs quantity by not having more treatments began the journey of frustration for the family like never before. Several of the children begged him to start chemotherapy again and begin the process of losing his hair again and all the other side effects it brings with it. No matter how much begging was done with him, he did not sway with his decision. There were many discussions with his kids arguing with him. It just made him more solid in his beliefs that he wanted to have the least side effects for whatever time he had remaining.

As the months went on, Richard became weaker and less capable of performing his activities of daily living. Hospice was discussed but he responded with his needs being met by Alice. He was not going to have strangers in his house to take care of him. His children did what they could which was very limited to bringing in dinners and picking up his favorite hot dogs from his ever frequented fast food place!

Financial issues started with the cost of his high-end medications that he needed for pain. He would decide if he wanted to pay for pain medications or save the money for other needs. His daughter that worked in health care for 20 years knew one of the most generous benefits of hospice was, medications used for the terminal diagnosis are free and paid for by the hospice provider. Richard swallowed his pride and signed up for hospice but would only let the nurse come in twice a month. He said no to other caregivers the hospice provider could offer. This financial help was a relief to both Richard and Alice as the months continued. As a family we were happy, he finally gave in and accepted hospice help when he realized the hospice benefit under Medicare A is fully covered and paid for all his pain medications and other prescriptions. The medications had become very expensive as his cancer progressed and his health continued to decline. This decreased the financial stress the family was feeling.

About two months before Richard passed away, his wife Alice succumbed to heart disease and ended up in the hospital herself. Richard accepted a home health aide for a night to help him with his cares while Alice was gone. The next day the hospice agency called his family to tell us the aide would never go back to our father's house out of fear. She had limited English capabilities but could understand him enough when he told her he was part of the Mafia and if she ever returned, he would have her taken care of!! She ended up spending the night in the bathroom afraid to come out!

Making an apology didn't seem like enough for that poor frightened caregiver who spent the night as far away from our dad as possible. He believed he was fine without anyone around. Talk about frustration on our part! He swore if he fell and died in the house overnight it would be just what he wanted. The kids discussed it and decided he had the right to die alone if he so chose.

One of the other benefits of hospice is covered medical equipment that will help in maintaining independence and the safety of the patient. We convinced dad to accept a commode for the bedroom and a walker to aid in his walking. Imagine our surprise when the delivery man came with these items and our father said he wasn't going to accept any of that crap because he didn't need it! We had no choice but to apologize and tell the delivery man to take the equipment back. The sad part is the frustration we as a family felt during this episode. This frustration did not register with our dad. He just turned around and hobbled back into the house.

The next month or two our father finally quit fighting the nursing visits and also allowed the chaplain to come visit. This is one of the team members of the hospice provider that is offered to all patients. Richard was exhibiting severe guilt over actions he had taken throughout his marriage in regards to financial decisions he had made, and the use of gambling to provide relief from his financial situation. He pulled away from God. He never thought he deserved to ask God for forgiveness because of the significant hurt he had inflicted on his wife and family over the last 45 years.

My father grew more weak and symptomatic with pain. He was able to go to the hospice inpatient unit for pain management. It took a few days for the pain to be under control. By this point, Richard had lost the will to survive. He was tired of fighting the battle against cancer. Richard decided to stop eating and drinking of his own accord. By this time in his journey, the children realized it was his decision to stop fighting. The family prayed for a peaceful and comfortable death.

Richard was on hospice at home for about nine months before he died, and the most distressing thing of all was the death of his wife 10 days before Richard died. It was an unexpected death and quite painful for the five children in the family. The hospice staff helped the siblings in their grief as best they could, as the family had to tell their father of Alice's passing.

The hospice nurses took care of him lovingly for the next two weeks while his body continued to shut down. During this time the hospice volunteers visited to provide support and companionship. Within a week after his wife's death, Richard went unconscious. His children took turns coming in every day to sit and support him along with his hospice team. Richard's family was very grateful to the hospice team, since he would accept help a bit easier from strangers who were trained in dealing with the death of their patients.

About a day before Richard passed, one of his daughters was there keeping vigil for a few hours. The hospice nurse came into the room to check on Richard and turned to the daughter and started a conversation. She said the volunteer wanted her to pass a message on to the family. During one of the last visits, Richard asked the volunteer to pray with him. Richard asked God to forgive all his sins. As they prayed, Richard turned his life over to God and told him he was his Savior. How does a family member say thanks for the priceless gift of salvation for their father?

His daughter had been worried about this precise thing and prayed for a miracle to happen so she would know in her heart that Richard was in Heaven. The tears that were shed during this conversation was proof of how important this message was to her. All the anger and frustration from the family was forgotten in those last moments before Richard passed in peace, thanks to the care of the hospice angels by his side.

Chapter 3

"My Plate's Not Full It's Overflowing All Over the Floor"

Dealing with being Overwhelmed

Linda

As a hospice nurse one strives to provide comfort, compassion, and dignity to individuals at the end of life. It truly is a privilege and honor to provide comfort for both the patient and their family during this stage of life.

The following story speaks to that privilege.

BR was an engaging woman with a large family. Her homelife had always been a busy one. As a younger woman she worked as a teacher, she raised a large family (10) children, and her husband traveled for his job. So, throughout her married life she shouldered quite a bit of responsibility in relation to her family. As her life evolved, she continued to have a household which consisted of grown adult children, her husband, and several grandchildren that were in and out every day. She was content in her life. There was only one issue in this peaceful yet active existence. She was diagnosed with a terminal illness which would eventually take away her ability to function independently. It would also necessitate her to require twenty-four care to meet her needs and remain safe in her home. This was devastating to her and her loved ones. She was the true matriarch within her family. She was the glue. She was the one to make sure everything that needed to get done, got done. What would they do without her assistance? This consumed her and this thought brought a sense of overwhelming worry to her. She continued to worry about her family and how they would manage vs. how she was going to handle the news she had been given.

Her physician made the referral to hospice. The doctor noted a significant decline in her ability to complete her normal activities such as preparing dinner and walking up and down stairs. She had several falls over the last few months, and she expressed increased weakness in her legs. Her family could not understand the quick decline in her functional abilities. BR was experiencing increased stress as she was not able to care for her family as she was used too. This put an increased strain on the family dynamics. Previously identified roles and responsibilities amongst family members would now need to change to help meet their mother's increasing physical needs.

When hospice admitted her, BR stated she knew her disease was getting worse. She needed more help in meeting her physical needs, such as walking and going to the bathroom. She understood that there was nothing more that medicine could do for her, and she would be completely dependent on others until her death. Her goal was to have a better quality of life. She wanted to be comfortable, and as independent as possible for as long as possible. She stated this was her expectation of hospice care. One thing was important to her as she participated in her plan of care. She wanted her family to be supported throughout her time with hospice and after she was gone. She smiled as she stated this; "I have taken care of my family for so long, and I was happy to do it. Not because it was my duty as a wife and mother, but because I loved them all so much. I am not sure how they will deal with things moving forward. I do everything around here all the time. My husband doesn't know how to do laundry, cook or clean, not that I would ever have wanted him too!" She felt her death would be hardest on her husband, as he was used to her taking care of everything.

Her plan was implemented and followed throughout by several members of the hospice team. Her daughters came over more and started taking on more of the day to day household needs. Her husband and sons were coping as best as they could, but still went to her even as she declined, for assistance and support.

BR's plan was a flexible and changing document that was revised as her health declined and her physical dependency on others increased. She remained an active participant in her care until she became unresponsive five months later.

Once she became unresponsive, hospice was in attendance more frequently supporting BR's needs and providing support and comfort to the family. One afternoon, when hospice was in attendance, she woke from her unresponsive state (we call this rallying) and sat straight up in bed. She looked around the room at the hospice staff and family that were there and stated, "Who are all these people? What are they doing here?" She yelled out her husband's name. She was totally exasperated stating "It is just like him! He invites all these people here, and does not tell me, and then expects me to entertain them! And then he just takes off! Well, I never!" At that time, she was trying to get out of bed stating, "It will just take me a minute to whip something up…… Wait until he gets back. We are going to have words. All these people, he always does this. I shouldn't be surprised!" With that final statement her daughters went to her and stated they would take care of everything and that she should rest. BR nodded her head, stating her daughters were great and she needed to rest. She laid back down, fell asleep and became unresponsive. She remained unresponsive through her death.

When her death was imminent, the hospice nurse and family members moved her bed to the window. The window looked out onto the lake. Her family stated it was her favorite spot. BR would sit and look out the window every day or when weather was permitting, she would be outside sitting and watching the sun reflect off the water. She once stated this was her time. Her quiet time before all the activities of the day took precedence.

The sun was just beginning to rise as hospice and the family moved the bed to the window. Her daughter opened the curtains to let the sunlight in the room. Her daughter stated it's your time now mom. As she took her last breaths her husband and the nine children that were present surrounded the bed where she lay. Their other child, who was out of the country, was on the phone placed by her ear. Each family member present, laid a hand on her body, told her they loved her, and stated lovingly she should let go, as they would be ok. They continued to tell BR that she had taught them well, and that they would take care of each other, as she had taken care of them for so many years. The sun light shone on her body as she died peacefully and comfortably with her family at her side.

Hospice was privileged to be present during this very personal end of life experience. Each end-of-life experience that hospice is a part of, strengthens the passion that each hospice nurse holds close to their heart as he/she continues to care for patients during these final stages of life. We all celebrate and prepare for the birth of a child; hospice assists the patient and family to prepare for the end of one's life. Hospice supports the family as they move forward in life without their loved one.

Chapter 4

I Live Between A Rock and A Hard Place

An Alzheimer's Story

Pam

One of the most heart-wrenching experiences I have ever known was helping a couple from our church family. I had gotten to know Ron and Julie over the years through church and through my mother-in-law. They were always such a nice couple. I helped out a few times when things got a little rough for them while caring for Ron's mother who was staying with them.

It started with this couple not coming to church so often any more. I wasn't quite sure why because it seemed so unusual. This couple was known to hold Bible studies in their home. Julie would attend women's Bible study at church where I would see her often. A very faith-based couple active with their church and church family.

Ron had owned a concrete company with Julie managing the office work. Ron is described by his son Ronnie Jr., as a "man's man". Ron was strong both physically and mentally, no one worked as hard as he did. He took his responsibility of caring for his family very seriously. Family was extremely important to him and he carried the burden of emotions both good and bad that were felt by any one of his family members. After retirement, Ron and Julie moved up north after friends from Chicago had moved here. They had three children, two sons and one daughter. Ron and Julie had lost their daughter and became guardians of her two children. They now were responsible for two of their grandchildren, Dan and Julie's namesake, Julia.

I have never seen a more openly loving couple in my entire life. Holding hands, sneaking in a little kiss, and always speaking life into each other. It was very apparent how much in love they were even as they reached their 80s.

This story sees the struggle of dealing with Alzheimer's Dementia from the eyes of both the inflicted and the spouse. We want everyone to know that this is a tough road but you are not alone. We hope through this story, you can identify with these struggles and find some satisfaction in knowing that others have walked this journey. Julie suffered from

Alzheimer's and Ron was truly caught between a rock and a hard place.

One day Ron and Julie asked me to stop by. They had something they wanted to talk to me about. Julie was very open and at this time was very aware that her "forgetfulness" was becoming more than just an annoyance. This was mid-summer 2018. She shared her concerns regarding going to church. She decided she would not go any longer, she was afraid she wouldn't remember the names of her friends she had known for so many years. This was an embarrassment to her and she did not want to put herself in that position. Ron was very supportive and could see the love of his life slipping and he feared what was going to come next. He feared this was going to become more than he could bear.

He was right and their journey through the course of her final months were hard. Ron asked me "what can we do". Their doctor had explained what the course would look like and prescribed medication to help slow down the process of the advancing dementia. Ron would say, "This can't be how it was going to end." "There has got to be something more we can do." I apologized for not having any clear answers for them except that my husband and I would be here for them and I could provide some local resources.

At first my visits were 1-2x per week. Julie would describe her memory lapses and expressed her feelings about knowing she was losing her memory but couldn't do anything about it. Ron made one thing perfectly clear that no matter what, Julie was not going into a nursing home. This was their home and neither of them were going to leave.

As time went on Julie's course took a fast pace. Oftentimes Alzheimer's can go on for several months or years, but for Julie we learned it was going to be months. From the time I started seeing them as a friend and giving advice where I could, it would be only months before Julie would succumb to her dementia. Ron, on the other hand, took a course none of us expected.

Ron was the rock, the person that made sure Julie was taken care of at all costs and at the expense of him if need be. Over time Julie started to remember less about the present and more about the past only. Behaviors started to become an issue and Julie would begin to sleep less. Safety concerns started to rear their ugly head.

The two sons from Illinois, Ron Jr. and Kevin were contacted and joined the rest of us in finding ways to keep Julie safe at home and fulfill Ron's wishes. Julia and Dan, the two grandchildren that finished growing up with Ron and Julie were faced with tasks and decisions that no one in their early 20s should have to deal with. My heart ached for the grown up realities they had already endured and the ones they were facing now. All the grandchildren had roles to play including Ronnie III and his sister Courtney who lived in Texas and Illinois respectively.

One day Julie got out of the house, ventured up the road to the main highway. A local resident stopped his car to see what

Julie needed. She was frantic and said there was a man in the house and he was trying to kill her. "Please help me." A police officer came, my husband James was able to get over there as his auto repair shop was very close to their home. Ron was beside himself and she did not know who he was and to her he was a threat. This event broke Ron's heart into pieces and began a long chain of heartaches. At this time, we learned that her memory and behaviors had escalated to the point and she was now not always recognizing family members. Ron was crushed. He could not get Julie to understand that he was Ron, her husband. He would never hurt her and he loved her very much. Oftentimes she would refer to Ron as his father, not as her husband.

This would go on for a while. In between thinking Ron was a threat and a very bad man she would remember Ron as her husband and become very lovable and affectionate with him. The dilemma was, this change could occur at an instant and Ron was afraid to do anything or say anything because he didn't know if at that moment Julie would remember him as her husband or not. I will never forget one time we were there and we entered the house and Julie said, "Good you are here". Ron looked at us and was truly broken. Julie went on to tell us we better keep an eye on this man because he is up to no good. "I don't know what he is up to but I am terrified of him and I am afraid he wants to kill me." "He may want to kill you too." "Won't you please take me home?" "I don't want to

stay here anymore," I just want to go home."
She couldn't tell us where home was but she
just knew it wasn't here in her own home.

The next few months looked like this.
The sons took turns spending a few days at a
time with Ron and Julie. Grandchildren Julia
and Dan were both recently married and Dan's
wife was expecting a baby. The typical work,
school, and all the things that occur when you
are newly married. We talked about getting
caregivers in the home. Ron was adamant. No
nursing-home. Locks, alarms and gadgets to
keep Julie safe were installed. Private
caregivers were hired to eventually stay 24
hours a day. Anything that could be
considered a poison had to be locked up.
Shampoo, soaps, medications, cleaning
products etc. Grandson Ronnie was over their

affairs but lived in Texas and did what he could to manage the estate money and determine how long this type of care could be sustained.

The private caregivers were struggling. Ron didn't feel they were taking care of his wife to the best of his wishes and Julie's on and off again behavior issues were wearing on them all. During these months, Ron's health declined. He had been to the doctor several times and to the hospital and emergency department for abdominal pain and nothing was found. He started to lose weight and become weaker but he would never give up on caring for Julie. Ron would go to bed at night with a flashlight so in case Julie got up during the night, which she frequently did, he could see what she was doing or where she was going.

Julie started becoming incontinent which meant she was having accidents and needed to wear briefs instead of underwear. I feel very strongly that God put me in their path for a reason because even at midnight if we got the call that Julie was having an "episode" we would go to their home and I could calm Julie down and make her feel safe again. Between her grand-daughter and myself nine times out of ten, we could get her to relax and agree to lay down again. Ron could not make a difference and it was more than he could stand. Oftentimes, reading a Psalm from the Bible would give Julie peace and take away her fears. I would hug her and tell her she is ok. We are here and are going to make sure you are alright. In Ron's eyes this was his job, but one he could not fulfill. Paranoia becomes very real with Alzheimer's Disease.

The times were not always bad. Looking through photo albums always helped her. We took rides and getting ice cream was one of their favorite things to do.

Julie started to have trouble walking and began using a walker. Eating was hit or miss and found we could get her to eat only if someone sat at the table and ate with her. Ron continued to lose weight and become weaker. James would have to carry him to bed at times as Ron could not get into bed on his own. He still clung to the flashlight and was prepared to help Julie if needed. Ron would ask the doctor what was wrong with him, but he received no answers after several trips to the doctor.

At this point I thought for sure she would be able to go onto hospice. More support, get some professionals on the case to help navigate these muckie waters. Medication adjustments were done but not much help. Julie did not qualify yet for hospice. We will discuss later in this chapter the qualifications needed for a dementia diagnosis for admission to hospice. When hospice came out to meet Julie to see if she may qualify, they were more concerned with Ron. That following week Ron was admitted to hospice and in a matter of a few weeks he passed. Julie would sit in the sun room and watch him in the hospital bed. She did not remember he was her husband but would show concern and say "I hope that guy is going to be ok, he doesn't look so good".

One of the funniest moments I had with Ron and Julie I will never forget. Ron was on hospice and he had a male nurse come and see him. Julie really liked him and said he was very professional. His name was Chuck. Later that evening I was there with his granddaughter Julia. Julie was talking about Chuck and said she would like to talk to him; she had some questions for him. It was a Friday night and we realized there was not a good reason to call hospice and we didn't think we would reach Chuck anyway. She insisted. By now we knew the signs of Julie's behavior escalating and she would become relentless and agitated until she got what she was asking for. It would be difficult to calm her down once her agitation escalated to a certain point.

Julia left the room and called her husband Justin. Justin was going to play the part of Chuck and we were going to call him and let Julie speak to him and ask her questions. We were trying to meet Julie where she was at with her delusions. Justin agreed and Julia came back into the kitchen where we were all sitting at the table. Julia took the house phone and called "Chuck" who Julie now called Charlie, and gave her the phone. The conversation went on for several minutes going back and forth asking Charlie about business strategies, billing practices, refunding policies, and it was clear she was back running the office for the concrete company.

Julia and I could not contain ourselves. We were giggling at the table and couldn't believe how well Justin was handling this whole phone call. After several minutes of trying to hide our giggling, Julie pounded her fist on the table and announced to "Charlie" that she had a couple of young school girls sitting at her table and they were obviously not understanding how important this phone call was. We had a poor regard for business. Julie scolded us and I had to excuse myself and leave the room because I could not contain the laughter any longer!

Some people might find this unsettling, but we knew Julie well. We also knew Julie's delusions. Her perceptions of her reality were her reality at that time. We needed to meet her where she was at and not argue or convince her otherwise. Anything that broke the tension in that home at that moment, and brought a little levity to the situation was welcomed in my book! Again, this was as real as it gets!

We truly believe Ron died of a broken heart. June 13, 2019 Ron passed. At the funeral I took the role of sitting with Julie so the other family members could participate in the receiving line and make sure they knew Julie was taken care of for the duration. She was sad but all of us were unsure if she knew at any point Ron was her husband and that he had passed. For the next few weeks we tried to keep Julie at home. She always asked for Ron. Where is he? When is he coming home? Why is he not here? This was so sad. Now that he was gone, she spoke more about him then shortly before he passed. She knew something was wrong and Ron, her husband was missing from her life. Many tears were shed trying to explain to Julie over and over again Ron was gone, and he is not coming back. She just didn't understand.

We got a personal care agency involved. Behaviors continued and we were looking at a geriatric psychiatric hospital to try and get behaviors managed with medication adjustments. I got a call one night from the caregiver around midnight and she needed me to come. As the caregiver was talking each word was interrupted with "ouch" or "stop!" We rushed over and knew something had to be done and despite Ron's wishes we could not keep Julie home any longer. A few phone calls later it was determined that Julie needed some professional help. There was a geriatric psychiatric facility in our state that specialized in treating behavioral concerns. The caveat was that to get her into this facility she would have to sign herself in. Even with the Power of Attorney for health care active and in place, without a "chapter" or being forced to go to the facility by authorities, Julie was required to admit herself. The plan was to drive her there and say they were going on vacation and checking into a hotel. Julie never questioned it, she signed herself in. The odd thing was that during her stay there she did not need any medication adjustments and on her own began to become more subdued and somber. Julie was then able to come home for a short period of time. She became too much care for one person at home, even with agency caregivers. She was very weak and now transferring with 2 people and we feared her legs would buckle and she would fall. The family struggled. They did not want to go against Ron's wishes. Finally, arrangements were made for admission to a local nursing home.

Julie spent a few months in the nursing home before her Alzheimer's was advanced enough where she couldn't speak or eat and feared choking. Julie was admitted to hospice and would soon be reunited with Ron. Julie passed on November 6, 2019 just five months following Ron. The family lost both their parents and grandparents in a matter of a few short months with several painful months that preceded their passing. I give that family so much credit for keeping Julie at home for as long as they did. This was not easy and required sacrifices by all. The Alzheimer's path is not a kind one. Just remember that during times of crisis and behaviors this is the disease and not your loved one. It is important to reach out and get support when you need it. You do not have to go on this journey alone.

Dementia of any sort is always a difficult road for anyone as well as the people close to them. There are many forms of Dementia. According to the CMS guidelines, (Government Regulatory Agency Centers for Medicare and Medicaid Services 2020) there are specific ways to look at dementia to determine if your loved one is eligible for hospice care.

Alzheimer's is treated a bit differently than other forms of dementia, because

Alzheimer's Disease has been determined to be a form of dementia that is terminal, so it can directly lead to one's passing. The challenge for families caring for a loved one with dementia is that behavioral and memory issues occur long before they are eligible for hospice care.

We must remember that a physician must agree that it would not be unexpected for someone to pass away in six months or less if the disease runs its natural course. This has to coincide with documentation in the clinical record to back up what the physician is saying. We will share the government guidelines in bold that hospice agencies must follow in order to admit someone to hospice care with a dementia diagnosis. These guidelines are taken from the CMS policy on hospice care for Dementia.

These guidelines are to be used in conjunction with the "Non-disease specific baseline guidelines" described in Part II of the basic policy.

1. Stage seven or beyond according to the Functional Assessment Staging Scale; We will address this scale in a moment.

2. Unable to ambulate without assistance; Must need the assistance of another person or use of equipment such as a walker or wheelchair to be able to walk or get around safely.

3. Unable to dress without assistance; Another person must need assistance with putting on clothes such as pulling up pants,

button clothing, help with putting a shirt on. Putting on socks and shoes.

4. Unable to bathe without assistance. For example, you may need help to get your loved one in and out of the tub or shower, along with physically assisting them to get cleaned up such as washing their hair, wiping them down, and helping them dry off.

5. Urinary and fecal incontinence, intermittent or constant; Is your family member or friend having accidents with urine or bowel movements? Do they have trouble knowing when they need to use the bathroom? I had a hospice patient with Alzheimer's Disease that always said she did not want to go to the bathroom. She always said she didn't have to go. It was a struggle to get her into the bathroom. Once we convinced her to get

up and go, (after a few choice cuss words) she would sit on the toilet and go. I always loved caring for the feisty ones!! Everyone one with dementia is different. Prior to hospice, the patient had been in the hospital with a severe urinary tract infection. Once on hospice, we put her on a toileting schedule throughout the day and she never had another urinary tract infection throughout her passing. We can't expect family to know all these things so we encourage you to lean on your resources, and use your medical team or our services to assist you with managing these types of issues.

6. No consistently meaningful verbal communication: stereotypical phrases only or the ability to speak is limited to six or fewer intelligible words. If a person is able to hold a conversation even if it doesn't make sense or

seems "made up" then they would not meet this requirement.

Patients should have had one of the following within the past 12 months:

1. Aspiration pneumonia; This is a type of pneumonia caused by someone having difficulty swallowing. When eating or drinking, food goes down the "wrong pipe" and gets into the lungs. Your lungs are not meant to have these "foreign" substances inside and so this becomes a source of infection and pneumonia is the result. A good indication that your loved one could be "aspirating" is if they frequently cough during or after eating or drinking.

2. Pyelonephritis or other upper urinary tract infection; This is a more severe urinary tract infection. A bladder infection is the most common type of urinary tract infection and

would be considered a lower urinary tract infection. When the infection travels from your bladder through the urinary tubes called "ureters", it can make its way to your kidneys. When the infection gets into your kidneys that is considered an upper urinary tract infection and is called pyelonephritis. This can be a more serious infection. It often means you have had a bladder infection for a while and untreated, the infection has made its way to the kidneys.

3. Septicemia; This is when you have an infection that could be a urinary tract infection, or pneumonia, or other infection in your body that has become severe enough to get into your bloodstream. This can be a very serious infection and some people do not survive it.

4. Decubitus ulcers, multiple, stage 3-4; These are bed sores that have gone beyond redness or looking like an open blister. You can see underlying tissue and sometimes it is bad enough to see bone. You may see black tissue in and around these wounds when they get severe enough.

5. Fever, recurrent after antibiotics; Fevers that return following treatment for an infection with antibiotics.

6. Inability to maintain sufficient fluid and calorie intake with 10% weight loss during the previous six months or serum albumin. This is often one of the first signs of decline when a person begins to lose weight without any explanation. The weight loss process goes quicker once a person is not able to take in enough to eat and drink. They may state they

are not hungry or just won't ask for food. Oftentimes during the course of dementia, someone loses the ability to cook and make themselves something to eat. Weight loss begins. Many times, in the earlier stages these people will continue to eat for some time if the meal is cooked or prepared for them and placed in front of them to eat. One suggestion is that if this is happening with your loved one, try to continue to eat meals together. Eating is very social and often the family member with dementia will continue to eat if everyone else is eating at the same time vs. having them eat alone.

Note: This section is specific for Alzheimer's Disease and related disorders, and is not appropriate for other types of dementia, such as multi-infarct dementia.

Part II. Non-Disease Specific Baseline
Guidelines (both of these should be met)

1. Physiologic impairment of functional
status as demonstrated by: Karnofsky
Performance Status (KPS) or Palliative
Performance Score (PPS)

2. Dependence on assistance for two or
more activities of daily living (ADLs) A.
Feeding B. Ambulation C. Continence D.
Transfer E. Bathing F. Dressing

Part III. Comorbidities- Although not the
primary hospice diagnosis, the presence of
disease such as the following, the severity of
which is likely to contribute to a life
expectancy of six months or less, should be
considered in determining hospice eligibility.

A. Chronic obstructive pulmonary disease

B. Congestive heart failure

C. Ischemic heart disease

D. Diabetes mellitus

E. Neurologic disease (CVA, ALS, MS,

Parkinson's)

F. Renal failure

G. Liver Disease

H. Neoplasia-Cancer

I. Acquired immune deficiency syndrome

J. Dementia

One of the tools used to determine how advanced Alzheimer's or any other form of dementia becomes, is the Fast Scale. The tool was developed by Dr Barry Reisberg. This scale takes behaviors as well as physical signs of dementia and places them in categories by severity. The official name is "The Functional Assessment Staging Test. This helps you and the hospice team to know when it may be time for hospice. Here is what the Fast Scale looks like. Keep in mind someone must be in Stage 7C or worse to qualify for hospice care. We understand that your loved one may need much more assistance before they get to this stage.

Stage: 1 No thinking declines. No subjective complaints of memory deficit. No memory deficit evident.

Stage: 2 Very mild cognitive decline (Age Associated Memory Impairment) Some examples might be: Your loved one is able to recognize that their mind may be slipping. They may be forgetting where they place things such as keys, glasses, or other familiar items. This individual might not remember names as well but to someone that doesn't know them they can appear to have a normal memory.

Stage: 3 Mild cognitive decline (Mild Cognitive Impairment) This stage is when memory loss becomes more evident. You loved one may have gotten lost driving themselves to the grocery store they have been to a million times. People close to them may clearly see there is something going on with memory skills. This person may have trouble finding their words now and then or are starting to have trouble expressing themselves. Learning or retaining new things are becoming more difficult. Recalling names becomes even more difficult. Someone in this stage may have "lost" their wedding ring (misplaced) and believe someone has taken it from them. This can be quite a challenge to deal with. Your loved one may be developing some "denial" skills during this stage.

Stage: 4 Moderate cognitive decline (Mild Dementia) This stage it is very obvious that memory deficits are occurring. Events may be forgotten, such as doctor appointment or other appointments that were made. During this stage it is apparent one can no longer work and be production. The inability to manage their bills and banking accounts will be obvious. During this time, they may be forgetting things about themselves. The positives at this point are that this person is usually understanding of day and time and recognizes familiar faces.

Stage: 5 Moderately severe cognitive decline (Moderate Dementia) A person in this stage can longer manage themselves without help. During this stage it is hard for the person to recall important aspects of their life. Their phone number or address of many years becomes hard to recall and often they cannot. They may not remember the names of their grandchildren, what school they went to etc. Usually, they can still remember their partner's and children's names. They still know who they are and can recall several things about themselves. During this stage they can still use the restroom and feed themselves but may have trouble choosing the right or appropriate clothing to wear.

These next stages are broken down in a little more detail.

Stage 6: Moderately Severe Dementia

o 6a: Needs help putting on clothes (developmental age 5 years old) They may be able to dress their upper body but may need help putting pants on or shoes and socks

o   6b: Needs help bathing (developmental age
4 years). Cannot bathe without physical
assistance

o   6c: Needs help using the toilet
(developmental age 3-4 years) Physical
assistance is needed to adjust clothing,
hygiene following using the bathroom such as
wiping, flushing the toilet, telling them to wash
their hands, and assisting with getting
underwear and clothes re-adjusted.

o   6d: Urinary incontinence (developmental
age 2-3 years) Here you will see urine
accidents. A toileting schedule may be helpful
here. Routinely taking them to the bathroom
may help manage this stage. Here they can
still say they have to have a bowel movement.

o   6e: Bowel incontinence (developmental age
2-3 years) A person in this stage now cannot

tell you when they need to have a bowel movement and accidents with stool occur.

· Stage 7: Severe Dementia-** Hospice appropriate. Will begin to lose the ability to eat or want to eat or drink even if fed.

o 7a: Speaks 5-6 words in a day (developmental age 15 months) Vocabulary is very poor. Often not speaking in full sentences other than using a couple words at a time.

o 7b: Speaks only one word clearly (developmental age 1 year) No or Yes or a name maybe all that can be said.

o 7c: Can no longer walk (developmental age 1 year)** Has lost the ability to bear their own weight. Now has become wheelchair bound. They can still sit up unassisted.

o 7d: Can no longer sit up without assistance (developmental age 6-10 months)** They can sit in a wheelchair but only supported with a pillow or something similar to help them sit up straight and not slouch over. Can't hold themselves up by themselves. Can no longer sit at the edge of the bed unassisted.

o 7e: Can no longer smile (developmental age 2-4 months)** Here they have lost the ability to smile. No talking. May be bed bound at this time.

o 7f: Can no longer hold head up by self (developmental age 1-3 months** They are bedbound at this time.

This is one of the most difficult diseases that has its effects on the entire family. Everyone feels the stress and despair dementia causes. If you or a family member is suffering from dementia, please reach out and get assistance and support as soon as possible. There are many local support groups for dementia. Here

is the website for the National Alzheimer's

Association: https://www.alz.org

Chapter 5: I should have, I could have, I would have

Dealing with Regrets

Linda

How many times have we thought that? Said that? As human beings, we have an innate tendency to reflect on certain decisions or choices we have made in our past, Asking ourselves "What if?" What if we could have made a different decision? How would that change things? Or would it have any effect at all? Some of those decisions leave an imprint on us; and can have either a positive or negative affect on future decisions.- With hospice you only have one chance to do it right.

AK had her first stroke when she was sixty-nine. She had her second stroke at seventy-nine. It was her second stroke that caused her death.

This story is about the last seven days of her life after her second stroke. The decisions that needed to be made and the need to promote a quality of life.

AK was brought into the hospital through the Emergency Room (ER) after developing symptoms of another stroke. She could not speak, was having difficulty swallowing, and was not able to respond to commands. She was exhibiting symptoms of acute anxiety. With her one functional hand she was picking at her clothes and bedding. She could not focus. AK suffered a devastating stroke which would leave her comatose with no quality of life.

Her family was not sure what to do. A plethora of information and options would be given to them from several different healthcare professionals. What was the right option of care?

She could eventually go home with twenty-four-hour nursing care and a feeding tube for whatever time she had left; she could go to a skilled facility and receive twenty-four-hour care there; or she could be provided comfort measures within an inpatient hospice, and let nature take its course. Her family knew that she would not want to live being totally dependent on others, so they thoughtfully decided to provide comfort measures.

This decision did not come easy. The family had strong cultural and religious beliefs. These beliefs had to be taken into account as decisions were being made. The eldest son wanted a second opinion. After all, his parents had lived with him and his wife for as long as he was married; and making the right decision would forever be part of his emotional future. He consulted with an outside medical group, and was told that his mother may or may not wake up, and because of this she will always need twenty-four-hour care. A feeding tube will always be needed, along with the potential of other complications due to her bed bound status. It was an emotional heart-wrenching decision made by the family. They would need to live with this decision for the rest of their lives.

She was moved to a different area of the hospital where her needs could be met in a comfortable home-like setting vs the aseptic nature of a medical unit. Physician orders were written for comfort care through in-patient hospice. Her family had encounters with social work for advanced directives, a chaplain to work through spiritual and emotional issues in collaboration with the family's Orthodox religious leader, along with nurses and physicians to provide an interdisciplinary approach to care.

The family was told by the medical team that if nature took its course, due to the severity of her stroke, she would pass away within the next two weeks. Hospice worked closely with the family to help them say goodbye and provide closure. This was important as this stroke came on suddenly and her imminent death was unexpected. The family had not been able to prepare physically or emotionally for this stage of their mother's life. There were questions, emotions, regrets, all intertwined with sadness and anticipatory grief. - Did we do the right thing? Should we have been more aggressive? Could we have prevented this? How do we say goodbye? Does she know we are here with her? What happens next? Is she in pain? Hospice's unique forte is supporting and walking with the family through this emotional rollercoaster. Helping them navigate through these questions, emotions and regrets are part of the hospice philosophy of care and continues for next 12 months after the loved one's death.

AK died peacefully and comfortably seven days later. Her family received support, and education throughout the last seven days of her life through the hospice team in collaboration with hospital staff. Hospice's calming and respectful presence validated to the family that they had made the right decision for their mother.

Chapter 6 "Hell No, I Won't Go!"

Dealing with Anger and Denial

Pam

In dealing with a terminal diagnosis, there is no "one size fits all". How you cope and accept the inevitable is different based on your personality as well as how you have dealt with other difficult decisions your entire life. For those people that have always created their own way in life, they can struggle with the loss of "control". They can't fix this like they have been able to fix other things. One way to deal with it is to just go on like it is not happening. Another way is to get angry. Anger is a natural stage of acceptance. There is no right or wrong way to accept your diagnosis and it is ok to get mad about it.

I will never forget the first time I met my father-in-law. He scared me to death! Quite intimidating to say the least but underneath all the gruff was a man with a kind heart. He loved kids but also loved to tease them unmercifully! The Dunwald men are quite the characters. Stubborn, headstrong, and very particular on how they want things done. They can be very colorful in explaining their point of view as the "right way" to do things. Get a few of them in a room together and you have a few "right ways" to do things and a very lively discussion. You know the saying, something about my way or the highway might have been an appropriate analogy. Just sayin.

Roy was a second generation mechanic. His dad, Roy also worked on cars and farm equipment and just about anything that needed to be fixed. My father-in-law and my husband who is the 3rd generation auto mechanic can fix just about anything and are very puzzled as to why everyone can't fix things because it is just good common sense! I say it is a gift, but I guess I may lack a whole lot of common sense because I struggle to fix just about anything.

When my husband and I decided to get married it was met with mixed emotions on his side of the family. When my husband James announced it to his mom and dad, Roy gave a big "Well I'll be damned". My mother-in-law was a bit skeptical and was worried about her son who had gone through a pretty rough divorce and wanted to know "What was so special about me?" Super uncomfortable moment but I lived through it. My mother-in-law and I have become very close. I just think she wanted to make sure I was going to stick around!

Fast forward 3 years to our wedding in 2003. It was small. We both love the "cowboy way" and secured a rural venue that was perfect for our "Western" wedding. We did everything simple as it was not the first rodeo for either of us. We talked about decorations, a live country band, flowers, how much we wanted to spend etc. On the day of the wedding as we were getting the old western town ready for the day's events, here comes my soon to be father-in-law with a bunch of wild flowers he picked all on his own for the table decorations. I was extremely surprised by the gesture but I felt very loved and welcomed into the family at that point!! You have got to understand my husband and his dad regard these flowers and all flowers for that matter as "weeds" and you must realize how much of a big deal this really was.

In fall of 2006 we moved here and James worked with his dad at Roy's Service, his auto repair shop with the plans of taking it over when dad completely retired. They were able to work together only a short while. Lively discussions and arguments were had over "where are my tools?" "I know you must have moved them, where did you put them?" "You have to do it this way." "No dad, I do it this way." These were common arguments heard in the shop and both ways worked but neither one would acknowledge that! Even so, no one would have traded those months for anything that James got to work with his dad.

Later that year, my father-in-law had open heart bypass surgery. He felt his recovery was never complete and always complained of "running out of air". He explained that he felt more short-of-breath after surgery than before. July 9, 2008 following a Bronchoscopy we got the news. These symptoms persisted and eventually led to a diagnosis of lung cancer, stage III and the oncologist gave a prognosis of 6-9 months to live without treatment. Treatment options were discussed and Roy declined further treatment of chemo and radiation and at that time it would entail an hour drive one way to the treatment center every day for weeks.

Slowly dad cut back on the time he could spend in the shop. He had to walk up a bit of a hill to get back to his house. He started taking longer lunches and then didn't go back down to the shop after lunch at all. Every day dad dressed in his work clothes. Soon he stopped going down to the shop altogether even if it was just to sit and visit with the customers while James worked on their vehicles. The end of the journey was near.

My in-laws heard of an American Indian doctor out west and asked if we would support them going and giving alternative medicine a shot. We agreed. This was August of 2008. The last thing we wanted to do was take away any hope. They had heard some good things about this man. They made their trip and dad endured cleanses and other forms of treatment. He came home and weeks later after sending an envelope of "spit" to the doctor he said he was cured. This was to the tune of $3500.00. By April 2009 things started to take a turn for the worse. Every day at their request, I would stop at their house on my way home from work to check on him and listen to his lungs. Desperately I wished I could tell them his lungs sounded better each day but after awhile they took comfort in me saying "no change" versus "they sound a bit worse today." During this time in April Roy started on home oxygen.

Roy, with his wife Lora's support, opted to enroll into hospice. This was in May of 2009. This seemed like the most appropriate avenue to take given his lack of desire for treatment. I was working acute care at a local hospital at the time and we made a referral to our hospital's hospice program and we began

the rest of the journey with hospice. A
hospital bed and oxygen were delivered and
the rest of the story begins. Nurse and social
worker visits became routine. Education was
received on how to give the morphine and
lorazepam in case they were needed. Dad
would need just a couple of doses
intermittently during his course with hospice.
He did not require much medication at all. Dad
could no longer go up the stairs to the main
living area where the kitchen and his bedroom
were. He was now confined to the basement
family room area. His shower was down there
and this is where family congregated to watch
T.V. so this for many reasons was a great place
for him to be.

Slowly his appetite became so poor he
would express it in anger to my mother-in-law

that she wasn't cooking anything he had a taste for. This was so hard for her to try and come up with something that he would want to eat. Every day my mother-in-law would ask him what he wanted for dinner. After a while, he gave no further suggestions. Lora tried to cook him his favorites and give him a variety. He would take a couple of bites and that was it. He just wasn't hungry anymore. He always said "it just doesn't taste good." This became the challenge of the day to try and find something he would eat. He did learn to like the Ensure chocolate and vanilla but only if they were ice cold. These became his main source of nutrition. The strong man I had learned to love was fading fast right before our eyes.

Roy passed away on May 11, 2009 and I will never forget the final 48 hours of his life. You hear stories in hospice about patients having a "rally day". This is where someone appears at death's door and all of a sudden, they are talking and things perk up and you wonder what just happened. We should have known that Roy would go out that way. It was a Sunday evening and we were all sitting vigil at his bedside waiting for him to take his last breath. His feet and legs were mottled. This is an eminent sign of death as the circulation winds down and the limbs furthest away from the heart start to turn a blotchy purple. We waited and waited. He remained unconscious but still breathing. His wife Lora was there, his daughter June and her husband Frank, James his son who is my husband and myself.

We are all surrounding the bed. All of a sudden Roy sits up, turns his head around and looks at all of us sitting around him and boldly says "What the hell is everyone sitting around here staring at!" The look on my brother-in-law's face was priceless, pure shock and disbelief! The next words out of his mouth were "help me get out of this bed I have to take a shit". We helped him up and he walked all by himself and used the bathroom and when he was finished, he returned to the bed and wanted to watch an old western on T.V. and said "what's for supper". I said let's call his other daughters. Roy and Lora also had twin daughters. Janet lived in Florida and Janice lived in South Carolina. Roy spoke to each of them and they were the most amazing conversations. Each daughter was able to say their goodbyes and have one last conversation with their dad before he passed.

Later that evening he fell asleep and never woke up again. Pastor came and visited that next day along with the hospice nurse. His brother came to see him as well as local talent who sang and played music for him. Roy remained unconscious and passed at 6:15 p.m. the next evening. We should have known he was going to go out on his terms his way. It was his way or the highway.

Death has no blueprint. Sure, there are signs and symptoms to indicate the end is near but we never know when that final breath will be taken. If you or someone you know is in a similar situation take every advantage of what time you may have left. You never know what moments might occur that may give you an opportunity for one last kiss, one last hug, or one last lively conversation!

Just as a note, hospice followed up with my mother-in-law for the next year. That was a rough period of time for her. She was most grateful for the grief support group she attended and she most liked being with the other wives that had recently lost their husbands. They could connect on the same level, understand each other, and share coping strategies in a supportive environment with the guidance of a professional. She talks today, about how much this really helped her through that first year.

****

Mr. Wilson

Pam

As a nurse, we all like a good challenge to take a gruff, unhappy frustrated patient and win them over. This is one of those stories.

Mr. Wilson had a respiratory disease that was terminal. He had been using oxygen at home for quite a while, but now leaving the home was getting too difficult. He just couldn't breathe. The dreaded "End Stage" words were used and he chose to accept hospice to finish out what time he had left.

We had a nurse leave and I would be assigned to take over his case. My first visit we didn't make much headway. He was quiet, stern, and not in the mood for any talking. He allowed me to complete my assessment, he answered my questions with only one word if he could, and agreed to the next visit.

Each visit we made a bit of a headway. He talked more, and I asked questions to try and get to know him and what he had accomplished during his life. Before long he started to ask me questions and we started to have real conversations. I learned he liked fishing. Well now we had some common ground to talk about other than his disease and how he was feeling. My family loves fishing, so I found this topic an easy one to participate in. Each year we have an annual fishing vacation where the entire family is "expected" to go. Needless to say, I had years of tales to share, and often Mr. Wilson's smiles turned into laughter. We talked about bait, tying your own flies, you name it, if it was about fishing we talked about it.

I started each visit with a fish story. If I had trouble coming up with one, I told Mr. Wilson it was his turn to start. He laughed and his smiles became more frequent. Before long, he told me he looked forward to my visits and our chats. Mrs. Wilson was happy to see him smiling and laughing.

One day Mrs. Wilson walked me to the door and thanked me for not giving up on him and appreciated me "buttering him up." I took the opportunity to ask her how she was doing. We had a long talk. Hospice is not just about the patient and meeting their needs, but meeting the family where they are at emotionally and helping support them. Taking care of the family as a unit and making sure everyone's needs are noticed and addressed are just as important to the hospice team. She had some things she wanted to get off her chest that she didn't want to discuss in front of her husband. She didn't want him to worry and she wanted him to believe at all costs, she was going to be o.k. From that point on, the end of my visit with Mr. Wilson started a new conversation with his wife, as I walked out the door.

One visit, the conversation moved from small talk and fish stories to what the dying process was going to be like. He finally had become comfortable with me that he could ask the tough questions. He agreed to use the liquid Morphine more and told me it helped him get his breath back after any activity. He became less worried about not being able to catch his breath. He wanted to know what to expect in the coming weeks. He knew his time was short and was worried he would not be able to stay at home for the duration. I asked him if something prompted all these questions regarding symptoms and what to expect. He paused for a bit and finally felt comfortable asking the question that was weighing the most on his mind.

Mr. Wilson was alert and not confused at all during this conversation. He remained sharp throughout. He asked me, "Why am I seeing people standing in the corner of the room staring at me? They scare me." I was a bit unsettled because I have heard of this phenomena often in the later stages of the dying process. We talked about the fact that this can be normal. Usually when a dying person sees people, it is usually family members that have passed before them. They are reaching out their arms as if to welcome them in. Time to come home so to speak, and it will be o.k.

Mr. Wilson never recognized any of these people but learned to accept seeing them now and then. One day I came for my visit and he smiled and said remember when we talked about seeing people standing in the corner of the room looking at me? I replied "yes". He said, "well, there is one right over there" as he pointed across to the corner of the room. I told him to "tell him hello" for me. He just laughed and we continued on with our visit. He told me later that he accepted seeing them as a part of the process and they no longer frightened him.

Within a week, Mr. Wilson needed more care than his wife could handle. The decision was to move him to the hospice house for his final days. His daughter came from out of town and there was some relationship mending that needed to occur before he passed.

I would continue to see him at the hospice house but in a short-few-days he became unresponsive. The day he became unresponsive, I had a full day of visits so I knew I couldn't get there before the end of the day. He was hanging on. I arrived and a few short minutes after I said my goodbyes he passed. His daughter thought he might have been waiting for me to say goodbye. He may or may not have, but I was grateful to get to see him before he passed.

One more hospice case. One more patient to get to know as a person. One more chance to make a difference in a person's life as they see the end of their life coming closer. One more chance to comfort a family and guide them through the grieving process.

Chapter Seven
My Life is One Big Pajama Party
Dealing with Grief

Pam

The social workers in hospice do a great deal of work in the area of managing grief. I have had numerous chances to observe them doing their amazing work. I can't tell you how helpful the social worker can be on a death call when you have anticipated that a family may not handle it well. Accepting the death of a loved one comes in many shapes and sizes. One size does not fit all. It is a process and every individual goes through the stages of grief at their own pace. Just a reminder, if you or a loved one cannot get past the grief seek help. If you feel your own life is hopeless or you feel helpless and have trouble functioning through the day-to-day routines of your life please seek help from a professional. There is no shame in getting help.

According to a WebMD article on grief and depression, the normal stages of grief are as follows: Grief & Depression Coping With Denial, Loss, Anger and More (webmd.com)

1. Denial, Shock, Numbness

This stage can actually be somewhat beneficial as our mind helps to protect us from a severe loss. Denial can serve us well to get through the funeral arrangement planning, and initial shock of experiencing the loss. We want to make sure we are not judging people by saying "Oh, they are taking this too well" "I can't believe they are not more emotional!" A good reason why it may appear this way is they are just in the first stage of grieving for a significant loss.

2. Bargaining-This is a tough stage. The person experiencing the loss may run things over and over in their mind saying "If I had done this, maybe he wouldn't have passed." "If she had just gone to the doctor sooner, maybe this wouldn't have happened." This is an important stage to work through and understand that it isn't your fault. If you get stuck in the stage it may lead to long term feelings of guilt.

3. Depression-During this stage the loss starts to become real. We are beginning to feel the impact of our loss. We may be sad, quiet, withdrawn, have issues with sleeping and not feel hungry. This is normal and means you are moving towards acceptance. There is no

quick way through these stages and everyone spends a different amount of time in each one before moving on. You can also experience shorter or longer periods in each stage as you move through the grief process.

4. Anger- You are almost there! During this final stage before acceptance, you may be angry about the person leaving you. Each person handles this stage in their own way. Grief may cause you to be angry just because you are now alone. You could be angry at the providers or the hospital staff. Maybe you had big plans in the works and now your plans are obliterated by the passing of your loved one. There could be a lot to be angry about, and you have to be able to work through it. Being angry at life itself along with just being miserable can be a part of this stage.

5. Acceptance- This final stage of grief is where the rubber meets the road. You have successfully passed through the stages of grief and you begin to come to terms with the loss. It doesn't mean you are jumping up and down with joy that "you made it!". These stages are fluid. You can move back and forth between the stages through acceptance.Completion of the stages and getting to acceptance means you are now trying to find ways to move on and start living again. This stage may not be an all or nothing stage. For example in the loss of your spouse, you may come to believe you are ready to think about finding someone else but you may not be ready yet for the actual process of dating. Just remember to allow yourself to experience the stages of grief and know that

this is normal. For example, my mother-in-law took a year before her life started to look somewhat normal again. She stopped going to church. She didn't want to leave the house. Her entire life was based on what she and her husband did as a couple. Now she finds herself alone and is faced with what her life will look like now as a life of one instead of two. What did help her was the grief group that was run by hospice where she got to meet other women that had lost their husbands and share in the grieving process knowing they were not alone. Her big thing was "no one understands what this feels like." Meeting with these other women who knew exactly how she felt brought great comfort to her.

In hospice we see all kinds of examples of dealing with grief. We see the grief even in their pets.

I remember one patient that I attended to during a night I was on call. This was not my patient so I didn't know very much about him or his family. We had a policy that when hospice staff would come pets should be secured in another room. This was a hard policy for me to enforce as an animal lover, but I understood the necessity for it. I found out the hard way why we had such a policy and why hospice may ask you to put your pets away when they come. One day I was visiting a patient who had five doxie mixes all in one large crate. The patient could hardly move, so when I was done with my visit, I graciously offered to let the dogs out of the crate for her so she didn't have to walk down the long hallway and let them out. BIG MISTAKE! I let them out of the crate and I had to run down the long hallway as they were jumping all over my legs trying to bite me. I even got a nip in the tush! The entire time the patient is yelling and screaming at them to stop. The barking and yelping were so loud all I could think of was I was going to be eaten alive! I was able to "pull it together"and safely get out of the home. I learned the value of that policy that day.

When I spoke to the daughter of the patient that had just passed, I asked if there were any dogs or other pets in the home that needed to be removed from the room. In my experience, dogs are very intuitive to death and share their own forms of grief. The daughter explained that they had a German Shepherd that was "dad's dog" but they would make sure he was put in another room. Dogs can get very protective when we attempt to remove the loved one from the room where they passed.

I arrived at the home to greet the Funeral Director that arrived at the same time. We went into the home with the equipment we needed to complete our end-of-life process. The process of cleaning up the deceased and placing them in the black body bag and loading them onto the gurney can be very stressful for the family and their pets. We suggest removing the pets, and we give the family the option to leave the room during this process. Some family members want to be present for everything we do and others want to leave the room because they cannot bear to watch the completion of this process. There is no right or wrong way only your way. One good thing about hospice is that in some states the hospice RN has authority to pronounce the time of death for the patient, and having the coroner come out for an expected death in the home is avoided. Please check with your hospice agency to see how this final process is carried out and what that will look like.

We were told that the patient was upstairs in the bedroom in their king size bed. We found him lying in the middle of the bed and I immediately saw their dog tucked away in the corner of the bedroom. I was surprised because they told me they would put the dog in another room. I questioned this and they told me they could not get the dog to move. They tried several times and he was too big for them to carry and they couldn't get the dog to leave the room. Best friends to the end, their German Shepherd was not going to leave his master. I saw this as a potential problem as none of us knew what the dog would do when we took our patient out of the room. The Funeral Director and I were both a little nervous.

We completed our tasks and it came time to take our patient out of the room. This took a while. I am only 4'10" and our patient was over 6 feet tall lying in the middle of a king size bed. I will leave it to your imagination to figure out what that looked like!

As we were leaving the room, we kept one eye on where we were going and the other eye on the dog. He never moved. This dog had the saddest look on his face I have ever seen on an animal. It was heart wrenching. We need to remember our pets grieve for the loss of their loved ones as well.

****

The last story I will share regarding the grief process was with a very special family. Most of our stories have been about older adults who have mostly lived a full life even though abruptly brought to an end by a single event or longer-term illness such as cancer.

I had the honor to serve a family of five. The three children ranged in ages from twelve to the early twenties. How this family rallied around taking care of their dad was just short of amazing. The middle daughter would sit next to her dad who had a brain tumor and play her guitar and sing to him. The oldest daughter took turns with mom to meet the personal needs of her dad. The youngest son struggled the most and to watch him go through the stages of grief broke my heart. Each stage was evident. From denial and asking for a friend to sleep over while his dad lies in a hospital bed in the front room for all to see, to never wanting to be home, and finally not wanting to leave his dad's side at the very end. No child should have to go through that but this is not the reality of life. I witnessed one family pull it together, financially make ends meet, divide household tasks while taking turns sitting with dad.

We said we were not holding back in this book so I want to mention one specific aspect of their story. With the brain tumor my patient struggled with seizures. His wife went along with all the recommendations from the doctors and did exactly what they said to do until one specific weekend. The seizures started at home. They would not stop. The seizures were part of his hospice diagnosis of a brain tumor so they could seek treatment for the seizures. Of course, this is considered a comfort measure as why would anyone be comfortable during a seizure. Eight hours later in the Emergency Department after several doses of IV medication to control the seizures he was able to go home. He went home on more frequent and larger doses of his seizure medication. His wife hated these medications because it made him sleepy and less interactive with the family.

She took matters into her own hands and began to look at natural more homeopathic interventions.

We are not endorsing any type of treatments in this book. Just talk to your hospice staff and they can help you look at all options. In this particular case, her methods of choice worked wonders in controlling the seizures and keeping him more awake and alert. She eventually took him off his seizure medications and just used her remedy to control his seizures. Again, please check with your health care providers before you take things into your own hands. We had many discussions with our medical director and at this stage of the game we all agreed she had the right to try.

This family fought for the way the dying process would go. On their terms, and that is the way it should be. I can't believe how many inspiring and strong families I have been able to meet and get to know.

Not all of the time does the grieving process allow for "designed path". A small handful of patients of mine no matter how many times I suggested the patient was getting close to passing the family never wanted to believe me. This usually led to a feeling of "unexpected" death and the grief process had an entirely different look. Acceptance took a bit longer. One daughter sought me out later after her dad had passed and thanked me for trying to make them understand their dad was dying. She told me she wished she would have listened. She would have made sure she was there when he passed. She expressed the guilt she felt for not being there when that time came for her dad.

This book can in no way help to predict how someone will experience the loss of a loved one. Grief has its own path. Some paths are longer than others. Our mind is designed to protect us. These stages are just some of the ways our brain goes to work to keep us safe in dealing with the enormous burden of loss.

Chapter 8

Is Your Number Up?

Pam

During my days in hospice, I never had someone question me regarding when the time was right to suggest to family that they contact out of town family members. Often if involved someone to make the trip back home to visit a loved one before they passed. This time was different.

Time was running out for my patient. He was sleeping more, and awake less. He stopped eating. He was now alert for just a couple of hours each day. I will never forget these two experiences that ended up being linked together.

I walked in to make my visit and since time was running short, several family members were often gathered in the kitchen to support their mom. I checked on my patient and we had a few words and he said he was tired and knew he didn't have much time left. I agreed and continued my assessment and asked how the pain was and if we needed to make any adjustments in his care. He politely said "no, I am ok". He had been declining fast and had recently stopped eating and just didn't have the will or the strength. He was no longer getting out of bed to sit in his favorite chair he spent so much time in during the last few months.

The Priest from the local Catholic Church was there to pay a visit and check in on how things were going. I was not Catholic but grew up in Chicago and had many friends that were Catholic and learned quite a bit about their faith along the way. Why am I painting this part of the picture? It is to explain that I felt comfortable around the Priest. I wasn't uneasy. I was looking forward to sharing in the family discussion with him until......

My patient's wife asked me a straight up hard question. One that we heard often but hated to answer. Our daughter lives in Alabama and she can't come home twice in a short period of time. She wants to come home for the funeral but could only spare ten days to two weeks with her job. Should she come now or wait? How long do you think he has left?

This is a loaded question, but a common one, and of great importance, and I wanted to get it right. I did my best to answer. Father turned to me and waited with baited breath to hear my answer. I didn't think anything of it, and used my best clinical judgement as an experienced hospice nurse, to give her an answer. My next words would end up haunting me forever and to this day the thought of this situation gets me fired up!

"Yes, she should come now. If she would like to have a meaningful conversation with her dad she should leave to come home as soon as possible. It is likely that he may not make it another couple of weeks." Father immediately got this angry look on his face and loudly proclaimed "Who do you think you are? No one knows when someone is going to die except for God! How dare you imply that you know when someone is going to pass!" For a moment I wanted to say "How dare you....." but I swallowed my pride at that moment and with respect I kept my mouth shut until after he left.

We don't have any crystal balls to tell the hour or minute someone is going to pass. I agree that it is not our place to decide. As a matter of fact, I had a patient that I admitted to hospice, and had packed up my things to leave as her sons helped her back to bed after she had a sandwich. We had a great conversation and she seemed to be doing ok. I left the home and didn't get 20 minutes away before they called and said she had passed. I turned right back around and went back. I for sure didn't see that coming! But for most people, there is a pattern and a process one goes through as they get closer to death. I have seen it hundreds of times. I learned the stages and often could determine if we were days or hours away. Not the exact day, not the exact hour or the exact minute. Father obviously didn't see it that way.

The family acted on my suggestion and the daughter came. She had a great visit with her dad and he passed before she had to go home. Is it so impossible to think that God is helping to guide the hospice nurse in making these decisions? I often prayed for guidance and as often thanked God for putting me in the right place at the right time with my hospice patients and their families. Another chance to make a difference.

Fast forward six months or so. I had another patient that went to the same church with the same Priest. It made me sick to my stomach that I would have to go through the same situation one more time with Father!

I always managed to avoid being there at the same time as Father or would excuse myself when he arrived for a visit. This family had a great relationship with the Priest and I did not want to do anything or say anything that would interfere with that.

The day came when I believed it would be my patient's last. I was teaching some of the grandchildren how to turn and reposition him in the hospital bed and administer medications to help keep him comfortable. He was unconscious and his breathing pattern had changed and I knew it would not be too long. The entire family was there and filled their living room. There was a lot of commotion and I was trying to make sure everyone's needs were being met amongst all the tears. From a distance I could see the son standing across the room and then it happened. I still had some things to take care of and anticipated having to spend quite a bit more time there before I could end my visit. The son calls out to me as I was helping to reposition his dad and says, "I think it is time we call Father." I don't know how but after 36 years of nursing I made the dumbest comment in my professional career. It was one of those knee jerk responses and as soon as he said that I shouted at the top of my lungs "NO!!!" You could have heard a pin drop in that house of a dozen people. The son stopped dead in his tracks on the way to the phone and looked at me with a huge question mark on his face and he could not believe I suggested he NOT call the Priest!

I quickly apologized and said by all means please do call Father it would be most appropriate. How could I have done that! It was such an awkward moment that I had to explain to the family why I blurted that out. At least they understood. I had built a great relationship with this family and they were able to laugh about it. Needless to say, I was packed up and ready to go by the time Father got to their home!

The great thing about hospice is when the nurse, social worker, and the rest of the team have time to get to know the patient and the family. You build relationships and trust. We can answer questions and be the person you can lean on. You can even survive a huge blunder like I did. When hospice is a "rush" at the last moment when everyone is in crisis mode, it makes it difficult to get the most out of being "on hospice".

When will your number be up? None of us know for sure. There are no rules, just guidelines. Everyone is different and walks their own path. No two deaths are alike, no two journeys are exactly the same. You walk your own walk at your own pace and hospice can be there for you along the way.

Chapter 9

Make the Pain Go Away

Pam

One of the most difficult and emotional hospice cases I had the honor and privilege to work on left me feeling helpless and powerless all at the same time. Those feelings did not stop me. Nurses and social workers are strong patient advocates as well as many other healthcare workers and providers. This day my advocacy would be tested to the limits.

We received a referral very late in the afternoon on a Friday. Hospice to start that night. Not a good time to initiate services. Limited resources are available after normal business hours let alone going into the weekend. Plus, the social worker and I were bringing a new hire out as a part of her orientation to hospice. It was a recipe for disaster but we didn't realize how bad until we got to the home.

This couple lived out in the middle of nowhere in the land of no cell phone service. Our patient's husband was a Vietnam Vet and fit the part of the Vietnam Vets we see portrayed in the movies. At first, I found him a bit scary and intimidating. His wife was to be our patient. She was nearing her end of life and in a great deal of pain. At the VA Hospital the only thing helping her breakthrough pain in between her oral doses of pain medications was Intravenous Dilaudid, or Hydromorphone, a strong opioid pain medication.

The husband whom I will call John, didn't care about anything in the world except making his wife comfortable and he was told hospice would do just that. Amongst the military paraphernalia, there was also a handgun out in the open and the scene itself was very unsettling. As we were preparing to do our admission paperwork and share information, John very bluntly says, "Before we do anything, I was told you could give her IV Dilaudid here at home, is that right?" That was never told to us in the referral by the doctor's office at the VA. We were not prepared to give her the medication he believed was the only thing that would help her and the only reason why he agreed to let us come. John had a bad experience with Home Health and felt they could not do what he needed them to do and felt it was a waste of his and their time.

We all looked at each other and as the nurse, it fell back on me to discuss medications as that was clearly my lane. I had to tell him we were not prepared to give him what he expected. We did not come with Dilaudid let alone a way to infuse it. John hit the ceiling and was so angry we all just froze while he yelled and screamed. He told us we were useless just like home health and why did we bother coming. All of us agencies are all alike, useless. We could just take ourselves and get the hell out of here. As fear came over all of us we wondered how we were going to professionally remedy this situation, then John did something I didn't expect.

This six foot plus man right out of the movie Rambo dropped to his knees, knelt at his wife's bedside and broke down in tears crying and telling her he will fix it somehow. That was it for me. He was broken and we were his last hope of letting go of his wife the way they had decided it would be. Truly a defining moment that melted the fear away and "fight mode" took over for "flight mode". There was no way I was going to leave the house and let him struggle on his own to try and make his wife comfortable and reduce her pain. She was suffering and we could see that but he insisted on taking her home. No more hospitals, no more institutions of any kind. He was going to lose her soon and it would be on his terms.

We now began the problem-solving process. I called the hospice director and when I couldn't use my cell-phone I had to use the couple's land-line. The problem with using

the landline is that I could not speak privately
and everyone heard what I had to say to my
"boss". As a patient advocate, right or wrong
this is what occured next. I explained the
situation to my manager and at first it was
said we couldn't give IV Dilaudid at home. In
my mind that was not the answer I wanted to
hear. I knew we used pain pumps at home to
give intravenous medications. I tried not to
argue but I was getting upset because I was
bound and determined to help this couple.
After a few minutes of going back and forth,
my manager asked me to find a doctor to write
the order. This would be difficult especially
within the VA system and being a Friday night.
The VA normally does not have a doctor on
call. I would need a doctor to give me the
order and a prescription for the medication we

needed. The second problem was finding a Home Infusion Pharmacy that would deliver on such short notice and accepted the VA as a payer.

I told my director "don't you worry about me finding a doctor to write orders. Please find me a pharmacy to deliver the medication." My manager was new in this position, feeling their way as the manager, and let's say much younger and less experienced than I was. This person certainly didn't know me very well if they expected me not to get my part done. With only the landline to use, I worried about the family hearing my conversations. I expected it would take a miracle to find a VA doctor. I asked my manager to take on the task of finding the infusion company. I would find the doctor. During this whole conversation everyone in the room heard the dialogue. The mood was tense to say the least. I called the VA where their doctors were located and of course the clinic was closed. I talked to the information desk and asked if there was a doctor in charge or on call. I just needed a bone. A little something to go on. The receptionist told me there is not an on call doctor and the only doctor in the building right now was the M.O.D. or Medical Officer on Duty. He was essentially the Emergency Room Doctor.

I was transferred to the ER and had the M.O.D. on the phone. I was persistent and pleaded my case. "Whatever you need, I'll do it, just tell me where to send the script", the doctor told me. Success, and now to call my manager and ask if a home infusion company was found that we can send the script to. I will forever be grateful to this doctor for seeing what my patient needed and having the compassion to do something unexpected in his role that night.

This conversation didn't go as well as the first and the first one wasn't so good either. My manager did not find me a pharmacy. It was assumed I would not find a doctor to give me orders. That was it, now I was over the edge. I couldn't speak to my manager any longer and I excused myself from the conversation before I said something I would regret! I was asked to call my manager on my way home because it was apparent I was upset. Upset, wasn't the word I would use to describe how I felt and what I thought of his leadership skills at that moment. Now, without an infusion company I didn't know when I would get home. I was not leaving until we had a plan in place.

John realized how much we were fighting for him and his wife. We didn't get the infusion set up that night but we did the next morning. John had some oral Dilaudid he could give his wife in pill form but the IV Dilaudid was the only thing that eased her breakthrough pain in between oral doses. He agreed to take the chance over night and we assured him we would be back in the morning with "the goods."

From that moment on, John knew he had an ally in caring for his wife. He developed trust in us over the few short weeks before his wife passed away.

One last time we would be expected to go the extra mile for John and his wife. The evening before she died, I was the nurse on call for our hospice team. I got a call to contact John as he had some concerns about pain management with his wife. I feel God puts us just where we need to be to make the biggest difference in people's lives when we are needed the most. He knows our skills, our strengths and our abilities. He won't give us more than we can handle.

I made a visit to John's home and his wife was struggling with pain. I contacted the doctor and he made some adjustments to her medications. He did not want to go in for acute pain management as he promised his wife she could stay home. One hour led to two, then to three, and four and so on. He was afraid to be alone with her and not be able to help her. We formally decided to use the benefit of extended hourly hospice care (otherwise known as crisis care, continuous care) in the home. I ended up staying all night as I was on call until 8:00 a.m. the next morning. During that night, I really got to know John and what he stood for and most importantly how much he loved his wife. I learned to both respect him and admire him for the way he took care of her.

I hated to go in the morning as I felt a little like I was abandoning him, but I knew my fellow hospice nurse on call after me would do a great job. I was exhausted. I needed sleep. His wife died just a couple hours after I left. I was told it was a very emotional passing and John did not take it well. I felt bad I couldn't be there for him.

A few months later as usual the sting of each death begins to pass and hurt less. It was time for our semi-annual memorial ceremony to honor all the deaths on our hospice service in the past six months. Often it is not a large gathering as people tend to move on and don't want to be reminded of the pain of grief during the last days of their loved one's life during our hospice care. Never in a million years did I ever expect to see John there. If I could pick out the one individual I cared for in the last six months that would not come, hands down I would say John.

After the ceremony he came up to me and we had a very brief conversation. He told me the reason he came. Since I was not present when his wife passed, he wanted to come and personally thank me for all the things I did to help them and to fight for what he wanted for his wife. I told him how much I appreciated him coming to tell me that and that I knew this was the last place he wanted to be. He chuckled and said I was right but it was important to him to thank me personally. I will never forget that case and I will never stop fighting for those that need a voice and cannot help themselves. Hospice nursing is hard. It was the hardest nursing job I have ever had. I can say with true honesty though, it has also been the most rewarding.

My manager and I ended up having a discussion the following Monday after the initial admission. Let's say I felt heard and it was acknowledged where I was coming from. We also understood each other, how we could have handled the situation better, and we were able to move forward. It was all good, and I would do it all over again in a heartbeat!

Part 2 Misconception #1

Isn't Hospice for People with One Foot Already in the Grave?

Pam

This for me is the biggest barrier we face as hospice nurses. Yes, a physician must certify that you have a condition, illness, or disease that if you passed away in six months or less it would not be unexpected. With that being said, Cancer is not the only diagnosis that qualifies for hospice. We will address that later. The biggest issue that I see, in my opinion, is that patients/families wait too long to explore the option of enrolling in hospice. Most, if not all hospice agencies can provide a consultative information only visit to explain what hospice is all about with no obligation.

What happens is that when all else fails and treatment is no longer an option then and only then will people consider hospice. The problem with this is that many hospice enrollments are done in crisis mode during the last week to days before an individual passes. The family and patient are distraught to have to accept their or their loved one's mortality. Things get rushed and everyone scrambles to get the resources in place to begin hospice care. This is not the best-case scenario. If you find yourself or a parent in a situation where they have an illness or disease that is not curable the sooner your loved one enrolls in hospice the sooner hospice can begin focusing on living. That's right, living. Hospice is a philosophy that no matter how many days you have left here on this earth hospice will help you live those days to the fullest. We are not nurses dressed in brown or black robes and carry a sickle and resemble the "grim reaper". More often than not we are called angels, clinicians who have helped bring peace to our patients as well as gently preparing the family to begin the path of grieving.

I will give you an example of one of my past patients. This is Cathy's story. Cathy did not have cancer but she had terminal illness Chronic Obstructive Pulmonary Disease or C.O.P.D. Cathy lived in the rural Midwest and her only daughter lived in the State of Washington. Cathy had a sister Jean in Florida. Cathy's only wish was that she could see her only living daughter one more time before she passed. Cathy had a hard life. She lost a daughter previously and had her grown grandson living with her. She was not easy to warm up to and she didn't trust anyone. I was not going to let that stop me. Through the cursing and the "F-Bombs" she dropped, we grew on each other. She learned that she had an ally, someone that she could trust and felt had her best interest at heart.

Cathy did not have many close friends as trust remained difficult for her. Her best friend and her sister were her main confidantes. Cathy would often "run things by" her sister Jean before making any decisions. One thing I did notice about Cathy, she always wanted everyone to think she was doing better than she really was. Her life now was living with her grandson and taking care of her two cats that were the joy of her existence.

As time went on breathing became more difficult. Cathy could not be without oxygen even for short periods of time. She used liquid morphine to recover quicker when she became short of breath with activity such as walking out to the mailbox with her oxygen on. Cathy used oral long-acting morphine twice a day to help her breathing over all. She had to find sedentary activities. Cathy chose adult coloring books. She colored the prettiest pictures with gel pens; sparkles and all! I still have a notebook from her with the most beautiful cover. I will always cherish it! Cathy and I shared our love of horses and the cover of the notebook, yes, a beautiful horse.

She had been on our service for about a year and we knew if she didn't make the trip to Washington State to see her daughter soon

it would be too late. She kept putting off
making arrangements and she finally shared
that she could not afford to go. Her best
friend agreed to accompany her on the trip
and assist in caring for her. Cathy's wish was
to travel by train. The problem was Cathy did
not have the funds to pay for the trip or a
plan as to how she was going to travel all that
way with oxygen. Oxygen tanks were not an
option. She would have to get a portable
oxygen concentrator she could easily carry.
This was going to be a ten day trip. As her
hospice nurse you better believe I was going
to move mountains to get her to her daughter.
Her daughter had recently had some health
challenges of her own and could not make the
trip to see her mom. Cathy had lost one other
daughter and was not going to leave this world

without seeing the only one she had left.
Hospice, her sister Jean and her best friend
made the trip possible.

Assembling all our resources and
contacting agencies that might help fund the
trip we wrote letters and anything we needed
to try and get her the money to go. The pieces
eventually fell into place. Those last couple of
months of planning, Cathy seemed to come
alive with hope and excitement. Cathy no
longer was focusing on dying but on getting to
spend time with her daughter and
granddaughter. Cathy kept in contact with us
during her trip. We arranged for another
hospice agency to fill in and be available while
she was there in case something happened. At
her hotel, an oxygen concentrator was waiting
for her. She didn't want to be a burden on her

daughter and thought it would be easier to stay at the hotel.

The trip went well but Cathy returned home exhausted, as expected, but fulfilled. I will never forget that day after she had returned home. I went to see her and she was in her bedroom looking exhausted. She looked at me with eyes that said "I quit. I'm done fighting." Cathy then spoke and said "It's time to go to the hospice house. Do you think they have a bed?" This surprised me because she always said we would have to take her out of there kicking and screaming because she was not going to leave her house. Her best friend had agreed to stay with her if needed when she could no longer care for herself. I knew at that moment Cathy was ready to die. She completed her mission and had nothing left to fight for and she was tired. We got her into the hospice house within an hour or so. Later that day she became unresponsive. Cathy passed two days later in our hospice facility. I will always remember Cathy and the joy we were able to bring her during the last couple weeks of her life. Had we waited to get Cathy onto hospice until her condition was such that it did not allow us to prepare to help her to the full extent of our capability, Cathy would not have been able to make that trip.

Cathy chose the way she wanted her life to look at the end. No fuss no drama she did not like attention drawn to her. When it was time to go, she quietly made her needs known. Another example of living life on your own terms for as long as you have.

Hospice is not for everyone. We understand this. Hospice is for those that do not want to continue to go back and forth to the doctor, back and forth to the hospital, undergo treatments that are making them so sick their quality of life diminishes. Please don't get me wrong. As an advocate, it is our job and our pledge to fight for what our patient wants. If it is to fight and to continue to seek treatment, by all means we encourage them to do so.

Please make sure that it is what THEY want and not just what the family wants. Have the courage to initiate the difficult conversation and find out what their wishes are before they cannot share them with you. We will address Living Wills and Health Care Power of Attorney during a chapter as written documents that can be prepared ahead of time to address the patient's wishes.

Having an informational visit prior to enrolling can help you and your family decide if hospice is right for you and If the disease or terminal illness qualifies you or your family member to begin hospice care.

Misconception # 2

Hospice Will Cost Me an Arm and a Leg

How Hospice Gets Paid For

Linda

Utilization of hospice revolves around two things. One, understanding the hospice philosophy and two, understanding how it is paid for. Lack of understanding in one or both of these areas will decrease utilization. This would be a true disservice to the individual who can benefit from its unique services.

This was true for MR. MR was approached over six months ago about receiving hospice services. MR had end stage heart disease and he had been taken to the Emergency Department four times in the last two months. He was told by his medical team that he had the maximum support he could receive for his diagnosis. There was no more that modern medicine could do for him. His physician discussed changing his course of treatment from aggressive to palliative. His medical team felt that he would have a better quality of life with changing his focus to comfort measures only.

MR became angry when the word hospice was mentioned. He stated- Isn't that where people go to die? And besides who is going to pay for it? I have too many medical bills now, I don't need another one! What can hospice do for me, except cost me more money?

These statements are all too common. They come from a lack of understanding of the philosophy and how the benefit is paid for. The following sections will hope to enlighten one's knowledge regarding this all-too common misconception.

The decision to start hospice for you or a loved one is a difficult one to reach. Once a family reaches that decision, the question then becomes where to turn for quality care you can count on. Asking friends or even your physician is one way to choose to find a provider that will help not only the terminally ill patient but the whole family. A suggestion would be to get information on at least two hospice agencies and ask both to come and discuss their services and what sets them apart from the other agencies. Compare services provided by each hospice agency. If the patient is declining rapidly there may not be time to do this. If this is the case, the other option is to use the Medicare website and find out what hospice agencies have good ratings and which hospices are not performing up to the standards set by the government.

On the Medicare.gov website, an individual is capable of comparing different hospice providers in their area. This feature can also be utilized to compare doctors, hospitals and nursing homes.
The Medicare Compare tool allows an individual the ability to make informed decisions as to health care providers.

The tool is easy to use and begins by signing into the Medicare.gov website (www.medicare.gov/care-compare/). You can choose what type of provider, such as home health, and hospice. You can also obtain information on skilled nursing homes. Once the type of provider is entered, you are given the option to put in a specific provider name. Information is shown on results from surveys taken by the families of the patients the hospice provider has previously cared for. You will find out if families would recommend this agency, how well they thought pain was controlled, quality of care, communication levels and other criteria Medicare deems important to rate providers on. Once a provider is entered and reviewed, you are able to enter another provider and compare the two agencies by the survey results.

Several categories of information are available on the website for patients and families. These categories include:

- What the hospice benefit covers
- How to file a complaint on a provider

· 　Questions to ask when you are interviewing different hospice providers to care for your loved one.

　　There is also a category of terminated or at risk for termination hospice providers from Medicare which allows a family to see deficiencies the surveyors have decided need to be corrected by the hospice. Follow up is completed by state surveyors in a given time period to confirm these issues are cleared up in a certain time frame. (Medicare.gov/care-compare)

Medicare / Medicare Advantage Plans
Medicare covers almost all aspects of hospice care with little expense to patients or families, as long as a Medicare-approved

hospice program is used. Nearly 1.5 million Medicare beneficiaries received hospice care in 2017, with services provided by nearly 4,500 hospice programs nationwide.

Hospice programs provide care and support people who are terminally ill. Their focus is on comfort, or "palliative" care, not on curing an illness. When a Medicare beneficiary enters hospice, the hospice benefits are provided under original Medicare, even if the beneficiary was previously enrolled in Medicare Advantage. [As of 2021, CMS will be piloting a program that will allow Medicare Advantage plans to include hospice benefits]. But if a Medicare Advantage enrollee who is in hospice care needs treatment for something that isn't part of the terminal illness or related conditions, they can choose to use

Original Medicare or their Medicare Advantage coverage.

To qualify for hospice under Medicare a patient must be eligible for Medicare Part A, and a doctor must certify that the patient is terminally ill and has six months or less to live. Medicare-approved programs usually provide care in your home or other facility where you live, such as a nursing home or, in some cases, hospitals.

Medicare hospice coverage includes a full complement of medical and support services for a life-limiting illness, including drugs for pain relief and symptom management; medical, nursing and social services; certain durable medical equipment and other related services, including spiritual and grief counseling, which Medicare typically doesn't cover.

There's no deductible for hospice care, and copays for covered medications related to the terminal condition won't exceed $5 (note that if a hospice patient needs medications that aren't related to the terminal condition, your Part D plan would still have to cover them with its normal cost-sharing requirements) and your medical provider has to notify the Part D plan that the medications are unrelated to the terminal condition. This can be complicated, but it's important to understand.

Hospice care continues as long as the hospice medical director recertifies that you are continuing to decline from your terminally illness. (MedicareResource.org)

Private Insurance

Most private insurance plans cover hospice care and other end-of-life care services. These insurance plans typically cover the full cost of hospice care, but each health insurance company may have its own set of requirements a patient must meet before they can begin hospice care.

At a minimum, most private insurance plans require that the patient be diagnosed with a terminal illness with a reduced life expectancy of six months or less. They also require that a patient discontinue curative measures before beginning hospice care, based on the overall plan coverage.

The majority of private insurance plans model their hospice insurance coverage on the federal Medicare hospice benefit program and may cover 100% of hospice costs. It is important to contact the insurance provider for specific details on what the patient's plan will cover and what costs the patient may be responsible to pay.

Medicaid (State) Insurance

The Hospice benefit is an optional state plan service that includes an array of services furnished to terminally ill individuals. These services include: nursing, medical social services, physician services, counseling services to the terminally ill individual and the family members or others caring for the individual at home, short-term inpatient care, medical appliances and supplies, home health aide and homemaker services, physical therapy, occupational therapy and speech-language pathology services.

Payment for hospice services is made to a designated hospice provider based on the annual Medicaid hospice rates issued by the Centers for Medicare & Medicaid Services (CMS), Center for Medicaid and CHIP Services. These Medicaid hospice rates are effective from October 1 of each year through September 30 of the following year. Payment for hospice care will be made at predetermined rates for each day in which a beneficiary is under the care of the hospice.

Individuals must elect the hospice benefit by filing an election statement with a particular hospice. They must acknowledge that they understand that other Medicaid services for the cure or treatment of the terminal condition are waived. Individuals may, however, revoke the election of hospice at any time and resume receipt of the Medicaid-covered benefits waived when hospice was elected (Medicaid.gov).

Disclaimer: The information is based on the most current knowledge and research to date.

Hospice Misconception #3
Don't give me the Morphine, You're Not
Going to Make Me Die Faster!
Hospice Speeds up the Dying Process
Linda

There are many myths associated with hospice care. One of them is that hospice will speed up the dying process through the medications that are utilized, or because the focus of care changes from a curative approach to a palliative approach.

This can be a hard misconception to change. As medications are used to ease the dying process, it can be a normal response to equate the continued use of certain medications (especially narcotics like morphine) with hastening death.

JC and his family made it very clear when JC was admitted to hospice, that he did not want any morphine. He did not want to be "out of it". He had heard too many bad things about morphine and he did not want it. His family was torn about his decision as two of his sisters were nurses. One worked in the hospital and one worked in home health. Each of them had brought to the table their own professional experiences with narcotics, especially morphine. They explained how it could help ease his pain and help with his breathing as his disease progressed. JC would not listen. He stated that the drug scared him. He stated he had taken many drugs for pain over the last few years since his cancer diagnosis. Nothing worked anymore. He felt that the amount of morphine needed to take care of his pain would kill him.

This just isn't true. Hospice is a type of care and philosophy of care that focuses on the palliation of a chronically ill, terminally ill or seriously ill patient's pain and symptoms. The hospice team are experts in pain and symptom management. Their innate ability to ease the symptoms associated with a terminal disease and the dying process are why hospice exists.

It is a focus of care for individuals who have learned from their Physician or Licensed Care Provider (LCP) that they are not expected to recover from their condition. It's about easing pain and helping families prepare for the end of life. Individuals in hospice care generally are expected to have less than six months to live if the disease runs its natural course. They're often at home, where family members and professional caregivers look after them.

There is no evidence that supports the idea that hospice or the medications they use to alleviate or control symptoms associated with the management of the individual's disease, speeds up the dying process. In fact, research suggests that using opioids and other medications to treat pain or shortness of breath near the end of life may actually help a person live a bit longer. Pain and shortness of breath are exhausting, and people nearing the end of life have limited strength and energy. So, it makes sense that treating these symptoms would increase the quality of life and might slow down the rate of decline, even if only for a few hours.

When a patient is receiving regular pain medication such as morphine in the final hours or days of life, there is always a "last dose". To the family at the bedside, it may seem like the drug caused or contributed to the death, especially if death occurs within a few minutes. However, this dose does not actually cause the person to die. It is simply the last medication given in the minutes or hours before the death naturally occurs.

Hospice and the interdisciplinary approach that is used, promotes a better quality of life. The quantity of an individual's life has already been determined by their disease process and prognosis. Bottom line, opioids and related medications often play an important role in maintaining the person's comfort and quality of life throughout an illness and the dying process, but are never utilized as means to speed up the dying process.

Misconception Number 4: I Will Be Left Home to Rot Because I Can't Go to the Hospital for Treatment
Being on Hospice Means You Can't Get any Further Treatment

Linda

One of the questions that come up often during an informational session with hospice staff and family is the questions regarding treatment. If I am admitted to hospice and I need to see a doctor for treatment I can't go.

Let's see if we can clear up some of these misconceptions. It is true when you decide to accept hospice care the selection is made to choose a natural course of treatment. The focus of care is comfort and quality of life vs aggressive curative treatment.

One must understand that if you get injured or become ill and go to the Emergency Department; your hospice nurse may meet you in the emergency room to discuss your treatment options. If something like this happens it is very important to call your hospice nurse first before you go to the Emergency Department. If you choose to get certain treatments you may need to discharge (revoke) from hospice so your treatment gets paid for.

Patients can discharge or revoke from hospice for a couple of reasons. First, you are admitted into hospice services, your symptoms are well managed, and you actually feel better instead of worse, or you do not continue to decline so you "graduate" from hospice. You can always be re-admitted into hospice at a later date if your terminal illness causes further decline. Second, you can ask to be discharged or revoke from the hospice.

If you are unsure about your desire to follow the hospice philosophy, you can choose to stop care and be discharged. You will resume your Medicare benefits or insurance carrier benefits prior to you choosing to select hospice. Going back and forth "on hospice and then off hospice" for short periods of time is not an acceptable practice for those participating in hospice. You always have the right at any point in time while receiving hospice to say "I don't want this anymore". You can then discharge yourself from hospice services.

The philosophy of hospice is to let your terminal illness take a natural course and allow for your symptoms to be well managed and keep you comfortable so you can enjoy every moment and live life to the fullest for as long as you can. Patients have received oral antibiotics to treat pneumonia or upper respiratory infections, or urinary tract infections (UTI), because the illness causes uncomfortable symptoms. Medicare has strict guidelines for hospice agencies to follow, and your agency will be able to answer any and all of these types of questions. Our point here is to let you know you always retain your ability to choose your care options, even when you choose hospice.

To address the philosophy of hospice a bit further, your doctor does have to attest that you have a terminal illness and it would not be unexpected if you passed in six months or less. That doesn't mean that you can't stay on hospice longer. After the six month period, hospice requires you to be seen and re-certified by your hospice provider validating that you are still continuing to decline. This process will continue every two months (60 days). No one can predict how long the process may last, but as long as you continue to decline you may receive hospice cares.

I encourage those that read this and have someone in mind that might benefit from hospice, to contact a local hospice agency and set up a time for an informational discussion. An R.N and/or a Social Worker will come to your home and explain all the benefits hospice has to offer. This is a no obligation meeting. It is an opportunity for all family members to get their questions answered so you can make an informed decision if hospice services may be right for you or your loved one. Services that are available with hospice include but are not limited to, R.N. visits, social worker visits as needed, aide visits to help with bathing and personal cares, Chaplain visits if desired, and volunteer visits to provide companionship. Some hospice agencies have enhanced services such as massage therapy, pet therapy, and music therapy.

The hospice team continues to be in contact with your regular doctor. Visits are adjusted and increased as your condition declines. Equipment such as hospital beds, commodes, wheel chairs, shower benches, and other items are available through hospice. Oxygen is covered by hospice, as well as your medications that are being used to manage

your symptoms and treat your terminal illness.

Misconception #5

Hospice Will Starve You to Death

Pam

This might sound really harsh but, accusations of starving their loved one is a real conversation we have had with many family members. We really need to address this because this fear is real. To the lay person not having the depth and breadth of knowledge around the medical and physiological education around the dying process, this is a great concern. To most people it is just common sense. If we don't eat and we don't drink we parish. This just goes against everything we believe as human beings. One way we care and comfort the sick and dying is to make sure they have food and drink.

Let us take the time in this section to explain the dying process and the natural changes the body goes through in preparation of dying gradually and naturally. As someone begins the process of actively dying, we can get to the point where "forcing" or encouraging food and fluids could be detrimental and cause more harm than good.

Many times, as we approach the end of our life our desire to eat or drink diminishes. The body naturally starts to shut down. The body starts its natural dehydration process. In no way are we recommending that a patient stop eating and drinking. We are discussing the person that has a terminal illness and they are actively dying. The patient has made the decision not to seek any further active treatment, and is choosing comfort measures only. We must respect their decision despite the pain and grief it may cause others.

Here are two examples of people I cared for that due to their terminal illnesses, they both ended up with tube feedings prior to going to hospice. Both women had strong wills to keep going. When the time came for hospice for each one of them, they wanted a chance to keep using their feeding tubes at the request of family members and themselves. I heard these words echoed twice. I don't want to stop my tube feedings. Conversations with the hospice team related to the benefit of tube feedings in relation to quality of life and end of life goals needed to occur. After these discussions were completed, both women and their families decided to continue with the tube feedings.

Both of the patients also decided not to have their feeding tubes changed if there were issues.

As time went on, both continued their tube feedings and gradually over time they asked for less feedings. This was because the amount of feedings were less tolerable. They became full faster and would get nauseated if fed too much. Gradually the feedings had to be discontinued. It had gotten to the point where the body was just taking the natural course and not requiring food. The body was beginning to shut down.

We can live quite a bit without eating but going without fluids will hasten the dying process. According to the article in Medical News today, a person with a terminal illness will begin to lose their appetite and eat and drink less as death approaches. This is a natural part of the process. The body is preparing itself to complete the final stages of this journey. It will be natural during this time that your loved one may urinate less frequently, go several days without a bowel movement requiring less and less trips to the bathroom and sleep more. A person may also lose the ability to control their urine or bowel movements. The body does not require as much nutrition when we are less active. It is not uncommon to sleep 12-18 hours and then even more as we approach this end stage of the process. The increased length of sleeping can occur as soon as two to three months before they pass.

If hospice is an option for your loved one, most agencies have a booklet that explains the dying process and what to expect. These publications are extremely helpful in understanding the normal stages and patterns you may see as you assist in the care of your loved one.

Oftentimes when we reach this point of slowing down the eating and drinking it is our body's way of telling us we have entered that final journey. As our muscles weaken, this includes all the muscles in our body and the muscles we need to chew and swallow. Swallowing becomes especially difficult and even if we gently try to get our loved one to eat or drink it may cause choking. With weakness in swallowing, it could even cause someone to "aspirate" or have food or fluid "go down the wrong pipe" and hence the food or fluids could go into the lungs and cause increased congestion, difficulty in breathing and possibly pneumonia.

The biggest issue we would like to address here is your concerns regarding this process. This natural process is often not painful. Pain could still be an issue depending on what is causing the dying process, but the natural process of eating and drinking less and leading to dehydration is not believed to be painful. Initially your loved one may complain of being thirsty and this is a real concern as this process starts. This symptom will pass in time. We want to make our loved ones comfortable at all costs. During this time while you or your family member still has periods of wakefulness, and is still alert enough to take in something by mouth, we have a couple suggestions that might be helpful.

Popsicles may be one good choice. Something cold like this can be both soothing and refreshing if they are experiencing thirst. It will dissolve more slowly and smaller amounts at a time can easily go down the throat with less swallowing effort than it takes to swallow a thin liquid like water. Sponge "toothettes", or swabs on a stick can be soaked in water and the mouth swabbed to keep it moist and decrease their feeling of thirst. Your hospice company will provide these for you if needed. Some families have used an eye dropper to put a little fluid in the cheek so it absorbs slower and doesn't run down their throat. Something as simple as using a straw, putting it into the liquid, and holding your finger over the top to plug the top end of the straw, allows a small amount of liquid to be released at a time, that also can be put in the cheek. At this point keeping the mouth moist will help alleviate the symptoms of thirst. This may be the best option for someone that is not alert enough or strong enough to swallow liquids.

We hope we have addressed some of your concerns around eating and drinking during the dying process. Nothing we can say here will help you get through the process of seeing someone you love get ready to leave you but what we can do is try to help you be as prepared as possible in knowing what to expect. No one likes to think they are ready for hospice or ready for their loved one to go to hospice. Hospice can be an ally in helping the entire family cope and provide safe and comforting care. Sometimes it's nice to know you don't have to go through this alone and you have someone to help see you through this journey.

Here are the resources we used for this chapter

https://www.medicalnewstoday.com/articles/320794

https://health.howstuffworks.com/diseases-conditions/death-dying/dying-process.htm#:~:text=During%20the%20dying%20process%2C%20the%20body%27s%20systems%20shut,wee ks%29%20before%20death%2C%20people%20eat%20and%20drink%20less.

Medically reviewed by Carissa Stephens, R.N., CCRN, CPN — Written by Lana Burgess on January 31, 2020

Hospice Misconception #6
"I am not ready to give up and you can't make me"
Hospice is Giving Up

Linda

Does being in hospice care mean that one is giving up? Some people believe when you sign on for hospice care you sign away your rights to just about everything--medical treatment, your personal physician, your ability to make decisions.

That misconception is far from the truth. One does not give up on living when hospice is chosen. In fact, hospice improves the quality of one's life, for whatever time they have left. This is done because the focus of care is on quality and comfort vs aggressive treatment. The disease progression will determine the quantity of one's life- but it does not have to determine the quality of one's life. One such instance speaks to our resolve as human beings. To live life on our own terms and die on our own terms.

RZ was definitely a man who lived life on his own terms. He did what he wanted when he wanted. He was not risk averse, so he took chances with his health and his way of life without worry over the consequences of his actions. He was diagnosed with cancer and was successful in keeping it at bay for about three years, but when it came back, it came back with a vengeance. It left him unable to work, in consistent pain, and with a decreasing quality of life. This angered him. He felt he was losing control. He was not going to let this disease beat him. He did it once, and he will do it again. He tried experimental treatments and therapies, but his cancer was winning.

Hospice was asked to speak with him regarding his focus of care. His medical team had spoken with him a few days before; letting him know that there was not much more they could do but keep him comfortable. They told him that he had weeks to months to live. When hospice entered the picture RZ was angry. He was not ready to give up the good fight. The "Hospice conversation" focused on RZs goals, his quality of life, because the cancer had already determined the quantity of his life. The hospice social worker and RN spent time listening to him and allowing him to express his feelings of hopelessness and anger. He was not ready to die. He still had things he wanted to do. Hospice explained that he was in control of this part of his life's journey. He was the captain and hospice, his medical team and loved ones, were his crew. The task was helping him navigate this journey. Toward the end of this conversation, he agreed to give hospice a try. He did this with the understanding that if this focus of care was not right for him, he would let hospice know, and he would be discharged to pursue other care options.

With that understanding, he consented to hospice walking this journey with him. He was with hospice for approximately six months before his death. During this time, hospice was able to manage his symptoms so he was able to improve his quality of life. He took a fishing trip with friends. Upon his return from his trip, he told his hospice nurse that he would not have been able to do that without the help of the whole hospice team.

Following that fishing trip, He decided he was going to clean out his shed, and he did. He remodeled the bathroom, painted the deck, and planted several new plants within his diverse garden beds. He was comfortable due to his pain being managed appropriately. Not that he didn't have bad days. He did. He got through them by resting and participating in his care. As the relationship grew between hospice and RZ, he felt more comfortable talking about his life, his regrets and his death. The hospice team helped him work through these issues so provide closure and peace.   RZ never gave up on his life. He continued to garden (his passion) until two days before his death. He spent time doing the things that were important to him. He maintained control over decisions related to his care until he became unresponsive. He told loved ones that he wanted them all to drink a shot to his life after he was pronounced dead. He stated he would be watching them.

RZ became unresponsive one afternoon after sitting outside on his deck looking at his garden (he left written instructions and a blueprint for loved ones on how to care for his garden after his death). He came in stated he wanted to rest, and for the first time utilized the hospital bed that was brought in for him. Prior to that day he stated that he was not going to use that bed until he was ready. The bed was by the window that looked out onto his beautifully pristine gardens. He fell asleep looking at his gardens and never woke up.

When his loved ones called hospice, they stated they felt it was his time. Hospice came and found his loved ones at his bedside; and a bottle of whiskey and multiple shot glasses on the dining table to honor his wishes when the time came. The hospice nurse told his loved ones that it would not be long, as his breathing was becoming shallow and his breaths were only a few times a minute.

Approximately an hour later RZ took his last breath. The hospice nurse who was at the bedside began completing her assessment to pronounce his death. Loved ones were already pouring out whiskey in glasses awaiting the pronouncement of his death. The hospice nurse was surprised as she listened at his chest. His heart was still beating. His heart continued to beat for five minutes after his breathing stopped. His loved ones stated they were not surprised by this. They stated he lived life by his own rules and he was going to die by his own rules.

Once the hospice nurse no longer heard his heartbeat, she pronounced his time of death. Every loved one present to witness RZ's end of life drank a shot to celebrate his life. A life that through the end was lived by his rules. A life that hospice was honored to be a part of as they helped RZ walk this final journey.

Chapter 7 "Oh No, Once You Get Me into Hospice There is No Turning Back!"
Once You Sign on to Hospice You Can Come Off

Pam

Uncle Harvey is the last of a dying breed so to speak. An old school cowboy in every sense of the word. He loves kids, fiercely independent and claims the only one you can rely on is yourself. Harvey is a great example of "living in the moment". He is never concerned about where his next dollar is coming from and always has some jingle in his pocket. He always lived carefree. Harv had an array of jobs he did as he moved about the country. He is kind and would give the shirt off his back if someone needed it more than him. You could always see him coming in his cowboy hat, boots, his winning ranch rodeo belt buckle, wranglers, and a western pearl snap shirt.

His choice of a rambling and drifter type of lifestyle left him with some burnt bridges as well as some horse deals gone bad. While Harvey truly has a love of horses and almost every paying job he had was associated with horses, these beautiful animals were also a commodity to be sold and traded and just part of the "horse business". His horse jobs included working many years on a local working cattle ranch as well as working as a stable manager for a Lipizzan Stable.

With Uncle Harvey's experience with horses, I felt he was more than qualified to find me a horse I would be compatible with. He chose that horse well and she is still with us today.

Amber is getting up in age but we shared a lot of miles together. I will always be grateful for my Amber and how well she took care of me in the saddle just as well as I took care of her. Thanks Uncle Harvey for making a great choice for us and being willing to give her up.

Harv had a significant horse accident that left him with broken ribs, a punctured lung and a crushed pelvis. He spent 31 days in a local hospital and was a non-weight bearing (could not put weight on his legs) for almost six months. He lived with us during that time so we could take care of him, as he was confined to a wheelchair during this time. Riding a horse after that became more difficult as the arthritis kicked in and weight bearing too early in his recovery. To this day Harvey still wants to deal in horses thinking some day he can ride again before it is too late.

Over the years Uncle Harvey's lifestyle and age took a toll on him. He suffered a heart attack and declined open heart surgery or stents. He just didn't want to go through that and was afraid he would come out on the other end worse than when he started.

We didn't realize how much Uncle Harvey had declined over the past year until he had a fall while stopping at the local Department of Motor Vehicles (DMV).

Harv was a mere 108 lbs. and twice in a two week period of time he was admitted to the hospital with aspiration pneumonia. He was choking on his food and it was going into his lungs. He was scared. After being discharged from his second hospitalization we had a frank discussion on how he wanted the rest of his life to look. He decided he did not want to go back to the hospital any more. He did not want to take his cardiac medications because he always got dizzy and sick to his stomach despite the changes in medications and dosages made by the doctor.

I spoke to his doctor and expressed his wishes. She wanted to set up a phone conference with Harvey to hear from him his thoughts. She also needed to explain the potential consequences of his decision and to make sure he was aware that these decisions could cause him to pass sooner. He wanted quality versus quantity at that point and with the doctor's blessing, we made a referral to hospice.

Being the flirtatious but harmless man that he always was, he welcomed any visits from the hospice staff but the reality was he was just plain lonely. He was no longer able to drive which meant he couldn't drive the Amish around, and this had become his social outlet.

Uncle Harvey didn't have many people he could rely on but those that he had all rallied to take turns caring for him at home. Since this happened in the middle of Covid, he declined a nursing home or the hospice house as he could not bear to be "cooped up in a place where I can't leave or have visitors". This put a burden on those that cared for him the most. Some were able to cook and make meals as their health didn't allow them to take care of him at his home. Others were taking turns spending the night as Harvey was afraid of staying at night alone and choking.

Over the next few months as people were fixing him three meals a day he would not choke on, he started to eat a little better. Pudding, mashed potatoes, mac n cheese, and similar foods became his required food choices and we provided his favorites and strived to get him a variety of foods he could tolerate. He had company three times a day for meals and someone to spend the night with him every day.

Every week the hospice nurse would come out and see how he was doing. The chaplain and the social worker also made routine visits. They arranged for a hospital bed, oxygen, an over the bed table, a special mattress for the bed, a commode and a shower chair. All this equipment was covered by hospice and available to him as long as he was receiving hospice service.

Over time as Harvey had all of this help in the home and he knew what he could eat and not eat, he began to feel better. While on hospice you have a six month period to see if you are continuing to decline. If you do not, or you improve then hospice is no longer an appropriate level of care for you. You do not necessarily have to pass at that six month mark but you have to show a consistent measurable decline in your condition. For example, a measurable decline might be seen in a continued weight loss, seen with an increase in your need for oxygen, increased pain that requires monitoring and medication changes, you are no longer able to tolerate solids, or an ongoing increase in weakness and a loss of ability to care for yourself.

During Uncle Harvey's initial six month period of hospice he gained 10 lbs. and needed his oxygen less and at rest was less short of breath. Even though his improvement is not dramatic it is enough to show improvement instead of decline. The nurse completes her assessment and looks at all aspects of his health and determines if he is declining, staying the same or getting better. We were given the notice that Harvey would be discharged from hospice. He graduated from hospice like many people do. With the increased services and care provided, he improved. He did not meet criteria to stay on hospice moving forward. Discharge due to lack of decline is not the only way someone leaves hospice services. If you remember my dad's story back in Chapter One of the first part of our book, you can also choose to sign out or revoke hospice on your own and reconsider it at a later time.

So, what now? Harv is off of hospice. His primary care provider resumed care for Harvey. Hospice scheduled a doctor's appointment and my husband took his uncle to see his provider. Harvey still does not want to go to the hospital. He still does not want to resume his cardiac medications. His doctor again explained the consequences of his decisions and that down the road hospice may become an option again. Another option of care that could be appropriate for him is Palliative Care.

Palliative Care helps people manage symptoms of their chronic diseases. Harvey still has coronary artery disease that is not going away. He is still at risk for aspiration pneumonia. Through Palliative Care, a nurse practitioner will come and see Harvey every couple of months to review how he is doing and will see him in his home. In between those in-home visits there will be phone calls checking in on him and making sure he is alright. Palliative Care will know when the right time is to re-initiate hospice.

You may be thinking what happens to all of Harvey's equipment now that he is no longer receiving hospice services? He does have to return them. Palliative Care can work with the doctor's office to have prescriptions written to obtain the needed equipment to stay safely in his home. Oxygen will not be provided at this time as he currently does not have a medical need for it. Under hospice, the oxygen is considered a comfort measure and can be provided as a part of hospice equipment and medications.

If Harvey would need any prescription medications his doctor will need to prescribe them instead of the hospice team. The same process he did prior to going into hospice.

Accepting hospice services is not necessarily a death sentence. It is a level of care that is appropriate if the doctor feels the end of life is approaching or if you have decided to stop any form of treatment for a terminal illness such as cancer. Hospice certainly does not give any type of impression that you can never leave hospice or that once you sign up you can never change your mind. You always have that choice. That really is what hospice is all about, it is giving you the choice to design your own end-of-life care. Just the way you want it. Hospice gives you the choice in how you want to live as well as how you want to leave this world.

Misconception Number 8

It's My Way or the Highway Don't Take Me Out of the Driver's Seat

(Maintaining control of your cares and end of life choices)

Linda and Pam

What Can This Journey Look Like for me?

Along this journey there is a great concern for losing your ability to make your own decisions. The perception is, once you have decided to enroll in hospice the hospice agency is now in control and you have gotten on a one-way train going somewhere. This could not be further from the truth. The most important pillar and the foundation of hospice is that you get to decide how your end of life journey will be lived; you decide where the train will go. You make the choice on how the journey is traveled.

There are many processes in place and resources designed to give you as many choices as possible. Hospice has volunteers to come and sit with you, play cards, read to you, or just visit. Volunteers donate their time to the hospice agency and get special training in helping patients and families cope with the dying process. Some hospice agencies provide music therapy, harp players, and other special services along with their chaplains, social workers, certified nursing assistants, and your R.N.s. You decide. You determine what that final journey should look like. There is no right or wrong way. No request not worth pursuing.

I had a hospice patient that enjoyed working on the farm with big heavy equipment.

One of his final requests made known to our hospice social worker was to get up in that bulldozer one more time and move some dirt. This would be no easy feat in his weakened condition. Hospice said let's make that happen. What do we need to do to help? Hospice helped his family make that possible. The men in the family gathered at our scheduled day and time and had to physically hoist him up in the dozer. They did it, it went well and the wish fulfilled. This is what hospice is all about. It's living the best life you can, for as long as you have. Going out your way.

One resource I was very glad to learn about was the specialty caregiver known as the End of-Life Doula. I had heard of a Birth Doula, someone that will sit and be the coach of a pregnant woman getting ready to deliver her baby so common sense would suggest what an End-of-Life Doula might be. I had the great pleasure to meet and interview Shanen Kazynski owner of Respite Caregivers of La Crosse, Wisconsin. I met Shanen through an online business networking group. She is one of the most professional people I have ever met and has such a big heart. I learned the End-of-Life Doula is another resource to ensure wishes are honored as life comes to an end.

Shanen has a passion for helping people especially those that have started the end of their life journey. It started when she was a teenager and she developed a strong drive to comfort those in need, especially those she felt were at risk to die alone. Shanen turned her compassion into a business. Some people are afraid of death, they are uncomfortable. Not Shanen, she looks at dying as an opportunity to honor her client and provide them with all the dignity possible while making sure their wishes are carried out and if desired, some form of legacy to leave behind for the family.

So, what does an End-of-Life Doula do? This is a paraprofessional who has had special training in end-of-life cares. This Doula can work along-side of hospice or independently. This is a private pay service that is separate from hospice. The family or patient most likely will pay an hourly rate for the doula. This caregiver is valuable to families that may need more hours of help then what a hospice agency can provide and can possibly be more flexible with their hours. A hospice agency can reach out to these caregivers and with family permission can be another resource for providing extra services.

A patient does not need to be enrolled in hospice to get the services of an end-of-life doula. This caregiver can be hired independently by the family and can provide longer term visits with the client or be called in at the last minute and provide personal care to her client after they have passed. Shanen takes great pleasure in offering all types of opportunities for a family to use her. You might find her recording memories or good bye messages, writing letters, helping the dying put together a legacy picture book, reading to her client, playing their favorite kind of music, holding their hand, just sitting and talking with them or just being there, period. Sometimes, just her ability to be there, so her client will never have to die alone.

Shanen shared a story about one of her clients. The family lived out of the area and their loved one was in a skilled nursing facility or commonly referred to as a nursing home. The family could not be with her and did not want her to pass alone. Shanen got the call from the facility that the person was believed to be actively dying. When she arrived at the facility, she was very disappointed to find her in a dark room with the door almost closed and no one was nearby. She was alone. Oftentimes, the dying are placed in another room away from the normal hustle and bustle of the facility to try to protect the morale of the other residents and provide privacy to the dying individual and their family.

Shanen quickly went to work to remedy the situation. Shanen was prepared. She had taken the time to check with the family to find out what type of music she liked and was prepared to play that for her. She sat by her and held her hand and kept her company. She talked to her. She was no longer alone. She was able to pass with the dignity and awareness that she was loved and cared for enough that she would not have to complete this final journey on her own. This is the beauty of an End-of-Life Doula and the simple things they do to make a big difference.

End of life also means funerals. In planning a funeral, you have so many options. One of the things we recommend is having a funeral trust. This is where you can sit down with the funeral director and make some initial plans or go all out and plan the entire process. You can pay for your funeral ahead of time and the funeral home will keep this money in a trust account to pay for your arrangements when the time comes. Planning the details ahead of time when emotions are not as high, relieves the stress and anxiety that the family is experiencing when the loss occurs.

Living Wills and Trusts are another way to prepare for the future and end of life. We encourage you to get in touch with the professionals that assist you in your financial plans to discuss the best options for preserving and dividing up your assets.

One of the things hospice can do for you is help you prepare an advance directive for health care. This document names the individuals that you choose to make your health care decisions when you can no longer make them yourself. You get to express your wishes. Expressing your wishes or "having it your way" comes right down to the funeral as well as other aspects of care.

We have a large Amish population in our area and three of the four neighbors that surround me are Amish including our closest neighbor.

The plains community is a great example of doing things their way when it comes to death and dying. Sometimes I think we could learn a lot from their simple and very basic ways.

There is never a question on how someone in their community will be taken care of. It is their duty to care for each other and I was able to see it first hand with one of my hospice patient's that was a member of our Amish Community.

Belinda had a brain tumor and her husband was wheelchair bound with a chronic muscle wasting disease. They still had several young children in the home that needed to be cared for as well as all the farm chores and cooking.

I had the rare pleasure of being welcomed into a community where most people are looking from the outside in. Over the course of our time on hospice together I learned a great deal about their culture. As Belinda became less capable of caring for her family their community assigned women and men to care for her and her family. Their oldest daughter took on the role of her mom sewing, cooking, canning, gardening, and caring for the younger ones. I would come early in the morning and sometimes see their daughter brushing the hair of her younger sister. I made the mistake one day of saying how beautiful her hair was and she became very shy and put her head down. Darn it! I forgot that one of the reasons there are no mirrors in an Amish home is that to admire themselves would be considered "vain" and not pleasing to God. That is why they do not want their pictures taken as well.

During my time with the family, I asked many questions. How does a couple decide to get married? What was the courting process?

I learned many things that both surprised me and those things that just made common sense. If a young adult, (the Amish finish school here at the age of 14, equivalent to our 8th grade) boy or girl are attracted to someone there is a process they must follow. Their spouse is not picked for them, as many people think. They have every right to choose. Sunday church gatherings as well as weddings and holidays are times when socializing occurs and they can meet other people in their community. If a boy or a girl writes a letter indicating their feelings towards another and they get a letter back, the courting begins. If no letter is returned with an accepting response, they need to move on to someone else! Great lessons were learned during these months!

Towards the end of Belinda's life, she moved to a family's home out of our area where she could have more help. I got word via a letter that she had passed.

The Amish have what is referred to as a "green" burial. They live in a time gone by but us English can learn a great deal from their community in caring for each other. It's funny that we have a modern term called "Green Burial," an environmentally friendly way to bury our loved ones. The Amish don't consider it a "Green Burial", it is just a normal burial in the every-day life of their culture. There is no embalming fluid used, their loved one is washed and placed in a pine box with a cloth tied under their chin to the top of their head to keep their mouth from coming open and set out on the front porch where it is cooler.

Funerals are arranged quickly. There is a small cemetery, or the family member may be buried on their property with other family members with no toxic chemicals being lost into the environment and no cement headstones to mark the graves. Sticks and natural materials are used as headstones.

Other ways to complete the end of life journey include, being embalmed in a sitting position looking like you are sitting down at the table to have a conversation with someone. I have seen all types of music, services in and out of church, communion served at a funeral, lunches, no lunches, etc. There is no right or wrong way to end your life journey; whether it is a Funeral or a Celebration of Life. It can be done your way.

One of the special simple things that hospice does for patient funerals is provide a single white flower. This is a symbol of honor, purity, grace, and provides a compassionate message left for the family. It lets them know we played a small part in bringing them peace, comfort through the end. A way for hospice to bow out, but telling the family we will take a small piece of their journey with us always.

For me, one of the most touching services I attended was the passing of a retired nurse. I have always enjoyed the servicemen and women who passed with military honors. There is nothing like the group of seven men and or women who each fire three shots in honor of their fallen member. That day I did not know there was an honor guard for nurses.

This group of professionals validated the true servant leadership that is the embodiment of the nursing profession. Clad in their nurse's caps, white dresses and tights, capes, a Florence Nightingale lamp, and a brief candle lighting ceremony hit home for me. This was a ceremony of honor. It only took about five minutes, and they recited the "Nightingale Tribute" along with placing a single white rose next to the casket to symbolize their dedication to the nursing profession.

According to my internet search, the Nightingale Tribute was designed in 2003 by the Kansas State Nurses Association as a special way to honor nurses at the time of their deaths. I have included the website as a resource for the pdf which explains how to use the tribute. nightingaletributeprogram.pdf

[(nursingworld.org)](nursingworld.org)

It reads as follows:

The Nightingale Tribute Reading

Nursing is a calling, a lifestyle, a way of living.

Nurses here today honor our colleague

_____ who is no

longer with us and their life as a nurse.

_____ is not

remembered by his/her _____ years as a

nurse, but by the difference he/she made

during those years by stepping into people's

lives, by special moments.

She Was There

When a calming, quiet presence was all that

was needed,

She was there.

In the excitement and miracle of birth or in
the mystery and loss of life,
She was there.
When a silent glance could uplift a patient,
family member or friend,
She was there.
At those times when the unexplainable needed
to be explained,
She was there.
When the situation demanded a swift foot and
sharp mind,
She was there.
When a gentle touch, a firm push, or an
encouraging word was needed,
She was there.
In choosing the best one from a family's
"Thank You" box of chocolates,
She was there.

To witness humanity—its beauty, in good times and bad, without judgment,

She was there.

To embrace the woes of the world, willingly, and offer hope,

She was there

And now, that it is time to be at the Greater One's side,

She is there.

I encourage you to reach out to their website listed to get all the information you need to implement this tribute to a "fallen nurse".

There are so many ways to pay tribute to a loved one that has passed. The important thing is that whatever type of service or program you choose, should be meaningful to you and the friends and family that will miss this individual. It should also be a reflection

of their wishes and how they wanted their end
of life journey to be remembered. How they
may, at the end, wanted to slide in sideways
and say "Man, what a ride!"

My Way or the Highway

Betty's Story

Linda

Hospice has taught me many things. The most important of which was being humble, and grateful for all the blessings that have been bestowed upon me. This lesson was learned from a patient that was diagnosed with terminal congestive heart failure. Her name was Betty.

Betty was a 52 year old woman who had just retired. She was looking forward to joining her husband in retirement and fulfilling their dream of driving cross country on Route 66. Her husband had a remodeled antique car that was going to be used for this adventure. They had a calendar with places and timelines all mapped out. This long-time dream was never going to be realized. Betty was hospitalized two days after her retirement for shortness of breath and chest pain. She had a long standing history of diabetes and heart disease. She remained in the hospital for two weeks. The first five days were in the cardiac ICU. The remainder of her hospitalization was spent on a cardiac unit. She came home with instructions to follow up with cardiology within seven days. After four days at home, she was back in the Emergency Department with shortness of breath and edema. She remained hospitalized for another week. She was sent home with a diagnosis of End stage (terminal) Congestive Heart Failure. She was told by the medical team that there were no further medications or treatments that could help her and she should consider hospice.

Betty was devastated. Her spouse was in denial of the reality of this diagnosis. She decided that she would entertain the idea of hospice, but she was uncertain whether it was right for her.

Members of the hospice team and I met with her and her husband on a Saturday evening. We had a long discussion about her disease process and her quality of life. She was grieving for what could have been. She never felt her life would take such a turn. She wanted to travel with her husband. She hadn't felt sick until her recent hospitalizations. She had been living with heart disease for the last eight years. This was unreal to her. She thought she had more time. It was her turn now. She raised her children, and had worked hard to get to her retirement. "This was not the plan" she stated as she cried.

She sat quietly and listened. She needed to be heard. My heart went out to her. By the end of our discussion she agreed to hospice, but only if her insurance would cover the cost. I told her that we had already checked into her insurance when we received the referral. I showed her the authorization form and explained what it meant in regards to hospice coverage. She and her husband were relieved to know hospice would be covered under her insurance.

She looked at her husband and stated she wanted to go on a road trip. She looked at me and asked if she could still do that? I told her we could discuss this further with the hospice team and determine what was reasonable, given her health and symptoms. Before I left that evening, her spouse pulled me aside and asked " How long does she have? Is it safe for her to go anywhere? Much less a road trip?" We excuse ourselves to Betty and went outside. I asked him what he understood about his wife's disease process, and what was he told by the medical team related to her prognosis? He stated he knew she was dying. He told me she was his first and only love. They had waited a long time and saved relentlessly to go on this trip. It was their dream, their time. They did their job, raised their children, and we're looking forward to time together. You could tell he was also grieving and scared he was going to lose the love of his life.

Based on the information provided to us by the referral source and discussions with the medical team; Betty had anywhere from three to six months to live. The hospice team and I had a discussion on how we could help Betty and her family grieve appropriately. They first had to deal with and adjust to this unexpected change in their life plans. Betty was admitted to hospice the next day, and was started on continuous oxygen. Our Nurse Practitioner went out to visit Betty to work with her on issues related to her cardiac status. A plan was developed to manage her symptoms and provide her with an increased quality of life for whatever time she had left in this world.

Betty still yearned to take a road trip with her husband. She knew she couldn't go across the country, but wanted to live out some part of their dream before she died. We enlisted the help of her husband. Together with the hospice team, we came up with a plan to allow her to travel (though limited), to an area within 300 miles from home. We established support from two other hospice agencies as she traveled through their service areas. This was no easy feat to accomplish. Timing and destinations, and hospitals with emergency access had to be identified. She also had to have access to oxygen along the way. These hospice agencies would provide assistance if needed since she would be outside our service area. They would be gone from our service area for two weeks. Betty was not aware of the planning. We did not want to disappoint her if we couldn't pull it all together safely. The day it came together members of the hospice team, myself, and her husband, told her the news and explained the plan. At first she was ecstatic, but then she became anxious. What if something happened? What if no one was around to help her? What if she ran out of oxygen? We sat and addressed all of her concerns. By the end of the visit she was going on that road trip!

One week later her and her husband were on the road with their beautifully remodeled antique car. She and her husband returned two weeks later. She looked healthier and happier. There were no incidents or trips to the Emergency Department. She told me later that day, that she and her husband reconnected and had formulated a new life plan while on the road. She further stated they were more in love now then before, if that was possible.

As the weeks went on, a familiar routine developed between the hospice team, Betty and her husband. Visits were now more frequent and longer in duration. We all could see her declining. She was requiring more and more medication adjustments to keep her comfortable. Her adult children were at the home more frequently. Betty was sleeping more during the day, but as soon as she knew one of her children was there she perked right up, talking with them or working on a craft project with them.

On a warm summer evening hospice was called by her distraught husband. He was trying to talk through his tears. He said I think it's time. Please come now. When I got to the home with the chaplain, Betty was barely responsive. Her husband was by her side, and her children were on their way. I worked to make Betty more comfortable. When her children got there they all said their goodbyes, and told her it was ok to let go. The chaplain was there supporting the family and assisting with any spiritual needs they may have had. Her husband then put a CD in with all their favorite songs. He got into the bed with her and pulled her close. By this time she was unresponsive. She passed two hours later in her husband's arms, listening to "their songs," her children by her side.

The Chaplain and I were humbled by this experience and this raw expression of love. Her husband stayed in that bed with her until the funeral home came to pick her up. We had a hard time separating them. He stated they had never really slept apart, how was he ever going to sleep again? The chaplain helped him into the other room, and stayed with him until the funeral home left with Betty. The Chaplain and I stayed with the family for a long time after that to help them with the loss of their loved one. When we left, we both realized that we had grown as servant leaders from this experience. We knew that when we laid down that night we could rest easy. We knew that we had helped in some small way to ease the end of a life journey for a fellow human being. Betty, who just wanted to live her life her way with the ones she loved.

Misconception #9 "You Won't Listen to My Family
When I can't Speak for Myself"
Making Your Wishes Known
Linda

It has always amazed me, how as we age, things that were important to us in our youth and young adult lives are no longer important. Now as our eyesight fades, and our waistline grows, one develops a new perspective on what is important to help one feel good.

My uncle is a great example of this change in perspective. Growing up I was in awe of this man. He was larger than life, independent, and lived an active life. As he aged and became ill his activity waned, and he became more frail. This was hard on his spirit. As it became increasingly difficult for him to remain independent at home, he decided to enter a skilled nursing home. He asked for my help. I solicited the help of my sister, a Licensed Clinical Social Worker to assist me in finding a facility / community that would meet my uncle's needs. His only requests of his new home were that the "place better have good food" and "I want a private room." My sister and I went on a quest. We researched the facilities/communities online, we looked at their staffing ratios, survey results, satisfaction surveys. This took about a week to complete. Then the calls to the facilities/ communities we chose (10 out of 30) to see if they had beds and inquired about the criteria needed for placement within their facilities/

communities. Once we had appointments we went on endless tours and asked our scripted questions. We wanted to choose the best place. We wanted to do right by our Uncle. We needed to make sure he was well cared for and engaged within his new home environment. He was going to enter the Skilled facility/community under hospice care, so making sure hospice was contracted in the facility/community we chose was also important.

   After it was all said and done, we chose a facility that had a contract with the hospice that was providing care to him, that was close to family, and had "good" food, but did not have a private room for him. He told my sister and I that it was ok but he wanted a private room. We explained that the number of private rooms were limited. They were used for residents needing medical isolation or were receiving rehabilitation services. He was admitted there until we could find him another community that met his requirements. He looked at both of us and stated "I don't think I am asking for too much. Good food and a private room." On reflection back to his younger years, this made sense. He was independent, single, and a private individual. So, my sister and I continued our quest. It was important to us that he be happy, and content in his new surroundings. Hospice had given us a list of other facilities / communities where they were contracted, so that we could look into whether they could meet all of my Uncle's needs. After a few more weeks of tours and paperwork; we found a facility/community that would meet all of his needs. Good food, and a private room. My sister and I were excited.

When we spoke to our uncle about this, he was chomping at the bit to leave. He did not like his roommate. He said the man kept his TV on all night, paced the floors and talked too much. We explained the transfer was set up for next week. He needed to be patient. His response was "I'm sick and I have only asked for two things. Good food, a private room. I want my privacy."

The day of the transfer could not come soon enough. The day before the transfer, my uncle's roommate passed away. My Uncle was upset. Not because someone died in his room, but because he died. This was a validation of my Uncle's mortality. My Uncle was afraid of his dying process. His demeanor became quieter and more introspective until the transfer happened the next day.

Once the transfer was completed, my sister and I were relieved. He was settled in a nice comfortable private room, and the menu looked great. What a relief! Everything seemed to be ok. He was settling in, he had been there two days and he had no issues, until- I received a call from him on a Saturday morning telling me loudly he wanted out. After several minutes of letting him vent and me trying to calm him down; the gist of the issue was turkey bacon! He did not want turkey bacon (or as he called it "fake bacon"). If he couldn't get "real" bacon he wanted out. Later that day, I contacted the facility and spoke to the administrator on call. It was explained to me that the facility/community catered largely to a population that requested Kosher food. So "real" bacon was out of the question. The administrator explained that turkey bacon was healthier. I informed her; that was not going to appease my uncle. He had never eaten turkey bacon in his life and he wasn't going to start now- at the end of his life. I was frustrated with myself. Why didn't we know this at the time we were touring? Why didn't we ask more questions about the menu? I told my Uncle we would look for another place for him, but it could take time. He understood, but was not happy. He told me to bring him a BLT club when I visited the next day. He stated that would help him until we found another place.

My sister and I were on the road again. Looking for another facility/community that would meet my Uncle's needs and serve "real" bacon. Three weeks later we found (we were keeping our fingers crossed) another place. The only issue was they did not have a private room at that time. They stated they would not have one available until the following week. By the way, the cost of the private room would be double what a semi private room would be, because they would not be able to put another resident in there. I explained all this to my Uncle. He balked at the extra cost of the room at first; but I explained that he had worked hard all his life. He saved and invested well. He needed to use it to take care of himself. This was his rainy day. He reluctantly agreed. He gave me this serious look and said "

I'm not going to be around much longer, I want a private room and good food while I can still eat."

De-ja-vu, he moved into another facility/community without incident. He received a private room and "real" bacon. What a relief! He was happy and content. When I asked him if he was happy with his surroundings; he stated: "I only wanted a private room, and good food. You gave me both. I'm ok."

As he became accustomed to his environment, Hospice made our family aware of his progressive decline. They encouraged us to spend quality time with him, they provided support and education to the family. The hospice team continued to allow my Uncle to determine his care choices even as he declined. Hospice was walking this journey with him and us. He maintained his dietary preferences until he could no longer eat. I spoke with the facility/ community, instructing them that I wanted to be notified with any change in my Uncle's condition. The hospice also received these same instructions. It was written on the front of his chart. I did not want him to die alone.

One night, when I was at home, I had a feeling I should call my Uncle. I dismissed it because it was late and I felt he would be asleep. Later that night, I received a call from the facility/community that my Uncle had passed and would I be coming in. I was angry and sad at the same time. All I could think of was that my Uncle died alone when I had instructed the facility/ community to call me with any changes.

When I arrived, the facility stated that he was awake at their midnight rounds, but, when they went to complete their 2AM rounds he was gone. I was upset. I felt I had let my Uncle down. Later, as I was waiting for family to come in, I was able to reflect on what happened. My Uncle was always larger than life. He was independent and did things his way. He was a private man and enjoyed his privacy. He lived life by his own terms and his death would be no different. He died the way he lived- because of hospice and his two simple requests he died with dignity, peacefully and privately.

Thank you, Uncle for allowing me the privilege and honor to care for you at the end of your life. Thank you for the lessons learned and quality of time I had with you to help you through this last stage of life.

There are documents that can be put into place to assure that your wishes are made known. Oftentimes the social workers at your clinic may be able to help you with a Power of Attorney for Healthcare at no cost. This indicates the person or people you determine can make decisions for you regarding your healthcare. Sometimes this is called "A Living Will". An Advanced Directive is a legal document that spells out the type of treatment you want as well as the treatments you do not want. This can be very specific and written in detail of how you want to be treated at the end of life.

Please ask at your next clinic appointment if you need help in initiating any of these documents. Your Estate Planning Attorney can also help draft these documents. You really can have control over what happens as life comes to an end.

Hospice Misconception #10- "I am Not Leaving this House"
Hospice Services Can Only Be Provided in A Hospital Or Other Facility

Mary

Can I stay home to pass away? This is another frequently asked question. I don't want to go to a nursing home. I want to stay home. I Am Not Leaving This House! These are statements hospice providers are often told by their patients. Getting a terminal diagnosis is difficult enough, but their emotional well-being depends on the opportunity to stay home and pass away within a familiar setting.

The beauty of hospice services is that they can be performed anywhere the patient wants to be. If the goal of the patient is not to go back to the hospital, a care plan can be written by the hospice team to keep the patient comfortable and help the family take care of their loved one. We need to talk about the different options of hospice care. The following information will provide you with a deeper understanding of the hospice benefit and hospice cares.

The hospice team includes a variety of people specially trained to meet the needs of your loved one. You have nurses, social workers, hospice medical directors, (doctor), chaplains, and others that may provide music therapy, pet therapy, and massage therapy. These resources are a blessing to the patient and their families.

One special group we would like to mention are the volunteers. These wonderful people go through weeks of training to equip them to be able to provide emotional support and other much needed services. These wonderful people do not get paid for their visits. They graciously donate their time. Volunteers may spend an hour or so at each visit with a hospice patient. These volunteers may be found playing cards, sitting and visiting, helping create a memory album, or any other non-clinical capacity that may meet a social need of the family and patient.

In order to meet the clinical needs of the patient there are options for the provision of hospice care:

1. In-home Hospice:

This is actually the most common and most often used service of hospice. Medicare covers the cost of hospice under the Medicare Part A benefit. You can choose to stay home and be surrounded by friends and family throughout your end of life journey. Hospice will provide all the necessary equipment and medications to keep you comfortable in your own home. A nurse will come to visit and visits will increase as your condition declines. A social worker will also visit as needed and will increase their frequency of visits as your condition declines. A Nursing Assistant will come and bathe you or assist with bathing, to make sure your hygiene needs are being met. The frequency will depend on how much you can care for yourself. In this scenario there must be an available and willing caregiver in the home such as a family member or friend 24 hours a day when it is no longer safe for you to be alone.

It has been my experience that many people can reach their goal of living out their final days in the comfort of their own home. If not, and it becomes too difficult to manage at home there are other options.

2. Hospice House or Hospice Residents Facility

This is a place where you can go and live and receive hospice care. Sometimes when you become bed bound, if it is too difficult to care for you at home you can request consideration for a "hospice house". An example would be if you live alone with your elderly spouse and the spouse could not turn and move you as needed. It may become too taxing to meet your needs

as more care is needed around the clock.
Medicare continues to pay for your hospice
services however, Medicare A does not pay
for your room and board to live there. This
would be your responsibility. Your hospice
agency could provide the details if needed. It
is important to note, some hospice agencies do
not have a "hospice" house.

3. Nursing home or Assisted Living Facility
You could continue to receive the same level
of hospice care as you did when you were living
at home, but again your room and board would
not be paid for and you would need to pay for
that.

4. Inpatient Hospice
This is usually at a hospital as an acute stay,
or within a freestanding inpatient hospice
facility. You would be admitted there due to

symptoms that are not able to be managed at home. For example, if your pain gets too bad and the hospice nurse cannot get it under control at home you may need to go into inpatient hospice to get it managed. Once those symptoms are managed, you could go back home with an updated plan of care and new orders to be able to manage your symptoms at home

5. Respite

There is a provision within hospice for Respite care. Respite care is a planned short break for the family caregivers, to get assistance from the daily care they provide their family members. It can only be provided at a Medicare certified inpatient unit that the hospice agency has contracted with which has 24 hour nursing care. The coinsurance is equal to 5% of the Medicare benefit that is paid and is owed for each day on respite care. Each hospice patient is entitled to 5 days a week of respite care each month. So, for example if there was a family wedding that you had to attend and no one was available to stay with you or your loved one; the hospice patient could have a respite stay in a contracted hospice residency. Your hospice agency could provide the details on how often that would be available.

6. Continuous Hospice or Extended Hours

When extensive nursing services need to be completed, usually close to the end of life, this is an option that can be provided. For example, at the end of life, if there were issues related to pain, breathing, and/ or comfort, the patient could be placed on this level of care. The nurse and other members of the hospice team would come out and provide "Continuous care" management until symptoms resolve. A nurse or aide may stay in the home for longer periods of time until the symptoms are controlled or until the patient passes away. This level of care can take the burden of caregiving off the family and let them just be there emotionally and physically for their loved one.

Medicare guidelines for hospice dictates the provider must offer bereavement services to the families for 13 months after a death. This might be in the form of phone calls, grief support groups offered to any family members who want to participate, and Veterans program for families whose loved one was a Veteran.

Durable medical equipment determined by need is covered at no cost to the patient. Some of the examples of equipment would be hospital beds, wheelchairs, wheeled walkers, broda chairs and oxygen. There must be a written plan of care that includes the items that were deemed necessary for symptom management. Delivery and pick up of the equipment are also covered free of charge to the patient and family. Supplies such as wipes and Depends are also considered covered items.

Medication coverage is another benefit for the hospice patient. The hospice agency provides all drugs and biologicals for the palliation and management of pain and symptoms of the patient's terminal illness. The patient will pay a coinsurance of approximately

5% of the drug cost for each prescription that is given while the patient is on routine or continuous care. The amount of the coinsurance must not exceed $5.00 for each prescription given to the patient. The same does not hold true for respite or general inpatient level of care.

The hospice benefit includes certain items to be included in the care once a patient is certified to receive it. There are no copays for the patient and the hospice agency is paid a per diem rate by Medicare for every day the patient is on their services. Ambulance charges that occur before the plan of care is initiated are covered under the Medicare benefit and not the hospice benefit. Once the plan of care starts, the cost of a transport is the responsibility of the hospice provider.

When a terminally ill patient chooses to stay at home and not be taken to the hospital, it is the duty of the hospice caregivers to do everything in their control to make this happen. Training can take place for the family members that are caregivers in how to keep the patient comfortable. There is support for extra hours for the hospice staff to be doing shifts in the home if needed. As a hospice provider their goal is to help the patient's end of life journey be peaceful, dignified, and comfortable. It is to support the patient and the family through bereavement to help them move forward without their loved one

The Blessing of A Volunteer

Mary

Do you remember the story of Richard? Yes, the Devil Wears Depends Hospice patient?. What a gift his volunteer was able to give my dad. How does a family thank a hospice volunteer for giving the gift of salvation to their dying father just before he passes away? It is difficult to do, but this will not stop that volunteer from helping out the next patient they are called to see and help at the end of the person's life.

The miracle with the volunteer occurred in 2004 with the admission of Richard into the inpatient unit of the hospice provider two weeks before his death. He was in the unit due to symptoms that needed to be controlled and the intense pain that was occurring due to the spread of the disease throughout his body. During his stay leading up to his death, he had a volunteer come several times who worked in the unit to help staff with emotional needs of the residents. Conversations were started in regards to Richard's guilt he had due to his lifelong gambling issues and all the harm and financial despair he had caused his wife and family over their many years of marriage. Richard had turned away from the church and God since he couldn't forgive himself. He knew God wouldn't forgive him either for all the pain he shadowed over his family for so many years. His salvation and path to Heaven was not deserved in his eyes no matter what anyone else felt or knew to be true.

The same volunteer came to visit Richard for several days before he became unconscious the last few days of his life. They had talks about the pain he had caused but also the love he had given his wife and kids for so many years. They discussed the meaning of forgiveness and how he just needed to ask God for it and once again declare God his savior and Heaven would be his to take. This didn't come easy for Richard but as the visits continued for that week the volunteer shared with Richard the gift of eternal peace.

As his daughter took one of the shifts to be by her father's bedside the days before he passed, the nurse came into the room and told the story of the volunteer and the visits they had shared on many of his visits. Forgiveness for Richard had been talked about many times and he had actually asked for it the last time the volunteer had stopped by. She said the volunteer wanted this family to know that their dad was going to Heaven and how it was an honor for the volunteer to be part of the beauty of his salvation. The joy his children have received over the years because of the kindness of this one volunteer is priceless. To think that situations like this happen so many times thanks to those who are willing to give of themselves without the hope they will get back something in return.

I Don't Want to Leave the House

Emma's Story

Pam

One special lady well known in the community was Emma. I met Emma through church. She and her husband were very active in our church and her husband continues to be today. Emma always sat in the pew next to my mother-in-law and I could always count on a hug.

Emma was well known in the community for having a huge heart for serving others. Not many people could say their lives had not been touched by her helping hand. I am sure there are so many stories that could be told. When I knew Emma, she was delivering meals on wheels. She took her responsibility very seriously and made sure everyone received their lunch. I have been told at one time she regularly drove four miles one way on a riding lawn mower to mow the grass of Ron and Julie's place before they moved up here permanently from the Chicago area.

We had a group of church members called "Hands of Faith" that would reach out and organize meals or other kinds of assistance. Emma was part of that group. She was known to visit members of our community that couldn't get out and just needed a friendly face to chat with for a while. If anyone in our area needed help of any kind Emma would know about it. She would give the rest of us the scoop so we could rally the troops and provide what was needed at the time.

We didn't expect that Emma would become one of our own that would need our help and support.

Emma asked if she could talk to me one day at church. I had heard that she may be ill but I didn't want to pry. Emma let me know she had cancer. She was very private about how bad it was. At that time, I was a hospice nurse and she was aware of what I did and where I worked. She didn't say much. She never complained about any symptoms or pain. She asked me when the time was right would I be her hospice nurse and provide support for her until she passed. She had one wish. She wanted to pass at home.

I promptly said I would be honored and gave her a big hug and in respect of her privacy I just told her to "say the word" and I will get the process and referral started.

Time went on and I watched her slowly decline. She never said much about it and never ever complained about anything. One day at church she said, I think I am ready. I asked her permission to contact her doctor who I knew well from my association with hospice.

The hospice admission visit was set and the ball was put into motion. I was going to be Emma's hospice nurse and I was going to fulfill my promise to be with her through the end.

Weekly visits in the beginning and so many nice chats. We talked about life as well as symptoms and if the medications were effective and made changes as we needed along the way. I met their son "Buck" and daughters Laurie and Dawn. Their devotion to their mom as things got a bit rough touched my heart. Her husband Lloyd would be there at every visit. He was so attentive and made sure he took notes, knew how to give the medications and wanted to know exactly what was coming next even when none of us were very sure. He liked to play cards but always scheduled his card playing around our visits so he wouldn't miss how I thought Emma was doing that day. I could always count on Lloyd having questions!

As we approached the last couple of weeks of Emma's life, Emma grew weaker and would get confused. It was hard to keep her down!! She was always on the go and slowing down was not on her list of things to do. Before long she gave into the rest part and was sleeping much of the day. During the night we begged her to ask for assistance to go to the bathroom and she was bound and determined to try to keep going on her own. Our aide visits increased to bathe her and make sure she was comfortable. Emma wanted to pass at home and we were going to make sure we did everything possible to allow that to happen and keep her safe.

One night I got a call. She had fallen. Emma tried to get herself to the bathroom which was about ten feet from the bedroom. Fortunately, she did not get hurt. I tried to reason with her but she insisted she was o.k. and could handle it. I asked her to please ask for help. She was a stubborn independent woman!

Lloyd did something that I don't know if many people would have done. This couple would easily be labeled "elderly." Lloyd was hard of hearing and at night time he would take his hearing aids out so it would be more comfortable to sleep. The problem was he wouldn't hear Emma when she was trying to get up. Lloyd knew how stubborn his wife was so every night until she no longer could get out of bed, he slept on the floor next to the bed. If Emma would try to get up out of bed, she would step on Lloyd first and he would wake up and help her. Now that is one devoted husband!

As the end approaches, there are often two paths the body can take. The system slows down and cools off or there is a short period of time when the body ramps up like you turned up the furnace. Emma took the second path. Her heart rate was elevated and she was extremely warm. We would use cool wash cloths to wipe her face and cool her down and after several hours of trying to keep her cool, she became unresponsive.

I was able to be there at the end and fulfill my promise. Quietly, peacefully, and with dignity, she passed. As a hospice nurse, it was an honor to care for her as she had so unselfishly cared for so many others in her life. God took home one of his servants that day. Emma passed on Sunday October 30, 2016 at home surrounded by her family. We made her request to die at home happen. Hospice was represented at the funeral with a single white rose that represents honor, purity, grace, and provided a compassionate

message left for her family.

Conclusion

Pam

We have done our best throughout this book to bring you the joys and heartaches associated with losing someone you love while traveling with them on their hospice journey.

Hospice may not be for everyone. We feel strongly however, that should that time arise it is an option that can add quality of life and peace of mind to the families. Hospice can help when the families are longing for support during this vulnerable time in their lives. It should be considered when no other treatment options exist or when your loved one just doesn't want to fight or go through treatments any longer.

We have shared stories with you that have touched our hearts forever. Stories that we still think about often along with the patients and families we have cared for. We shared many laughs and tears while putting these stories to paper.

Hospice nurses are challenged with cumulative loss, and the emotional effects of several deaths over time. I couldn't sleep at night and dreaded when my phone rang. Death is something you get used to but it never impacts you less. Each patient and family are different. Each person impacts you in a different way. If you are a hospice nurse reading this book, we admire you, as you are a very special person. Make sure you take care of you, and when death gets cumulative seek help and take advantage of your hospice agency resources.

Please remember to thank a hospice nurse. Our reward is not the pleasure of our patients getting better, but the satisfaction of being there when the road is rough, to ease pain, and provide comfort. This is one of the true essences of nursing.

It has been our pleasure to bring you our first book as we take you along with us as we launch "Your Nurse Advocate Consulting, LLC".

If you would like to learn more about our services and how we may assist you, please visit our website and share your email address with us. Feel free to add a message on your specific needs or questions. We will also provide you with a free checklist you can use to help you determine if the time has come when your loved one needs more help in the home.

We leave you with this poem. It was written by Pam almost three years ago. It is truly a summarization of a day in the life of a hospice nurse.

A Hospice Christmas

By Pam Dunwald

Twas the night before Christmas our bags are all stocked

We will answer our phones any hour on the clock.

We won't deliver toys, good cheer or a new pair of gloves

But you can count on our comfort, support and unconditional love.

We focus on life; quality not quantity is our

voice.

You begin your last journey but the "how" is

your choice.

Our wish for you this upcoming New Year

is that we alleviate pain, suffering and fear.

You miss your loved ones their voice and heart,

But all of us need to focus on beginning a new

start.

Hold onto the memories that is the key

For they are in a much better place we all

must believe.

So, our wish for you this very night

Is that you hold on to your loved ones so very

tight.

May each day bring your sorrow towards rest.

Just know it has been our honor and privilege

we all feel so blessed

to care for your loved one in us you do trust

and meeting your needs is an absolute must.

So, for all the husbands, wives, sisters,

brothers, and children too

To all a "Good Night" and may God Bless You.

Resources

CMS.gov

https://www.medicalnewstoday.com/articles/320794

https://health.howstuffworks.com/diseases-conditions/death-dying/dying-process.htm#:~:text=During%20the%20dying%20process%2C%20the%20body%27s%20systems%20shut,weeks%29%20before%20death%2C%20people%20eat%20and%20drink%20less.

Medically reviewed by Carissa Stephens, R.N., CCRN, CPN — Written by Lana Burgess on January 31, 2020

https://www.alz.org "When to Start Hospice care- Consumer Reports"

Kansas State Nurses Association

nightingaletributeprogram.pdf (nursingworld.org)

Medicaid.gov

Medicare.gov

Medicareresource.org

Webmd.com Grief & Depression Coping With Denial, Loss, Anger and More

Made in the USA
Monee, IL
11 March 2021